Everything You Always Wanted To Know About Serial Killers (But Were Afraid To Ask)

Mason Ryan

Everything You Always Wanted To Know About Serial Killers (But Were Afraid To Ask)

Other books by Mason Ryan:

The 100 Deadliest Serial Killers

The 100 Deadliest Female Serial Killers

Contents

What Are Serial Killers And How Many of Them Are There?

FBI Investigator Robert Ressler is often credited with coining the term serial killer. The term only really entered the general lexicon in the 1980s. The FBI generally states that one must kill three people to qualify as a serial killer. There must also be a gap between each killing. A bomber, for example, is a mass murderer or terrorist as opposed to a serial killer. According to the Crime Classification Manual, a serial murderer is defined as 'three or more separate events in three or more separate locations with an emotional cooling off period in between homicides'. This classification is very flawed though because, according to its strict criteria, Dennis Nilsen (who murdered at least a dozen men) is not a serial killer! Nilsen only killed in two separate locations.

It is often said that serial killers fall into four distinct groups. Visionary, Mission-oriented, Hedonistic and Power/Control. Visionary serial killers are the ones who, when captured, say that voices in their head told them to do it. They believe they had some divine or mystical mission to murder people. Peter Sutcliffe (aka The Yorkshire Ripper) was an example of this type of killer. Sutcliffe (who suffered from paranoid schizophrenia) said that God told him to kill prostitutes.

Another example of a Visionary serial killer would be Herbert Mullin - who killed thirteen people in California from 1972 to 1973. Mullin also had paranoid schizophrenia and believed that he had to murder people as part of a blood sacrifice to prevent earthquakes from happening in California. He started to hear voices in his head which told him the only way to prevent earthquakes was human sacrifice. A Mission-oriented serial killer will target one specific type of victim. These killers have a desire to punish and eliminate one specific section of society. An example of this type of killer would be Sergei Ryakhovsky. Ryakhovsky is known as The Balashikha Ripper.

He killed at least eighteen people in the Moscow area between 1988 and 1993. Ryakhovsky said his mission was to cleanse society of homosexuals and prostitutes.

Another Mission-oriented serial killer would be Steve Wright. Wright became known as The Suffolk Strangler after he murdered five female prostitutes in eastern England in 2006. The source of his descent into madness seems to have been his alcohol and gambling addictions - which left him bankrupt and suicidal. Steve Wright's victims were all prostitutes. The youngest was only sixteen. He killed the five women in only five days - a rate which made him a prolific killer by any standards. Luckily, he was caught quite soon into his killing spree. Wright clearly had a grudge against sex workers and wanted to kill as many as possible.

The Hedonistic serial killer will murder purely for their own pleasure. The gratification can come from the financial rewards of killing (like stealing money and valuables from victims) but the main motivation for this sort of killer is sexual satisfaction. There are many examples of this sort of killer. Jeffrey Dahmer is often classified as a Hedonistic killer because he lured male victims to his apartment and then sedated them to satiate his warped sexual fantasies. Dahmer would even eat parts of his victims. Dahmer had strange and unfathomable urges and desires which he couldn't stop himself from fulfilling - no matter how horrific and harrowing they were. He couldn't control himself.

Power/Control serial killers get their biggest thrill from the dominant feeling they get from killing someone. Ted Bundy, who obviously falls into this category, once said that murder was about possession and dominance rather than violence or lust. These serial killer categories can overlap. Take Dennis Nilsen for example. Nilsen is one of the worst serial killers in British history. Nilsen confessed to murdering fifteen men from 1978 to 1983 and said he tried to kill others. Dennis Nilsen's motive for murder was almost identical to Jeffrey Dahmer. Both of these notorious figures said that they killed because they didn't want the men they had met to leave them. They both, in their warped way, decided that being with a dead person was better than being alone.

Nilsen admitted that he used to talk to the corpses of his victims as if they were still alive and then sexually abuse them. Nilsen's MO was remarkably similar to Dahmer but Nilsen clearly loved the power and control that his murders afforded him. Dennis Nilsen said he used to get a sexual thrill from watching the limbs of a dead victim dangle around. He hung his first victim from the ceiling until the dead man's fingers were grazing the carpet. Nilsen loved the sense of power that having a dead body as a 'toy' gave him. You could say that Nilsen was both a Hedonistic killer and a Power/Control killer. The modus operandi of many infamous serial killers matches the Power/Control theory. Many killers will handcuff or tie their victims up and even torture them. They love the feeling of having someone helpless and completely at their mercy.

Thankfully, the chances of you walking past a serial killer in the street or encountering one in real life are slim to say the least. There really aren't that many of them compared to the general population. Scientific American said that serial killers only account for 1% of the yearly murders in America. The FBI once estimated that serial killers are responsible for about 170 murders a year in America. As there are thousands of murders a year in America, serial killers account for a very small number of victims. It is estimated that 15% of serial killer victims were chosen at random and just happened (unfortunately for them) to be in the wrong place at the wrong time.

Not all serial killer murders are random though. There have been many murders by serial killers where they already knew their victims. Serial killers will even do surveillance on potential targets. Before his gruesome attack on the Florida University Chi Omega sorority house in 1978, Ted Bundy hung around the campus and even drank in some student bars. He was essentially doing some research before his harrowing attack. Bundy was clearly storing information about the geography of the campus and the movement of students at night. This sort of research is far from unheard of when it comes to serial killers. Lawrence Sigmund Bittaker and Roy Lewis Norris became known as The Tool Box Killers after raping and killing five teenage women in California in 1979. They lured the women to a van where they would then rape and torture the victims before killing them. The evil duo staged a few 'test runs' at first where they approached young women but did not abduct them. This was their research and preparation for the crimes they would later commit.

Most of the very famous serial killers eschew guns because firearms destroy the intimacy of murder. Guns are still the most common method of murder though when it comes to serial murder. Radford University's 2016 report found that 42% of serial killer victims were shot. 21% were strangled and 14% were stabbed. Radford University's data suggested that only 7% of serial killers murdered their victims by means of poison. A study once claimed that a serial killer's method of murder is related to IQ. A smart killer will use a gun while a stupid one will be more bestial and primitive and use a knife or their bare hands (or in some cases anything blunt object that comes to hand). This study doesn't make perfect sense though because killers with fairly high IQs like Dahmer, Kemper, and Bundy, were amongst the most gruesome killers. Aileen Wuornos, who was no rocket scientist, always used a gun. A knife is the most common component of a serial killer kit. Rope and tape is not far behind.

Though some killers have expressed remorse for their crimes, many experts doubt that serial killers are truly capable of this emotion. Dennis Rader (aka The BTK Killer) said he once gave a victim a glass of water when they said they felt sick. These little flashes of 'humanity' in serial killers have been documented before. In his confession, Jeffrey Dahmer said that when he cut up his victims he would remove his clothes and place the victim in the bath. He said he felt brief remorse for the victim but this did not last. Mostly, he felt excited.

Because they don't have normal human emotions or feelings, serial killers tend to see their victims as mere objects to do with as they please. The fact that they are causing pain, suffering, and death doesn't bother serial killers. They don't worry about things like this.

Ed Kemper was one of the few serial killers to give himself up to the police. It is very rare for serial killers to turn themselves in. Some killers do though seem to experience a sense of relief when they are caught. Dennis Nilsen seemed to be relieved when he was captured. Kemper and Nilsen had both had enough of the real world and the ghastly and grisly circumstances of their lives. They both seemed to deduce that prison couldn't be any worse. Nilsen is quite rare among serial killers in that he allowed some victims (who he could have killed if he desired) to live. Usually when a serial killer does this it is a more self-serving and pragmatic form of 'mercy' than the one shown by Nilsen.

The Hillside Stranglers (Kenneth Bianchi and Angelo Buono Jr), for example, once let the daughter of the actor Peter Lorre go rather than kill her. They only did this though because they calculated that murdering the relative of a celebrity would bring too much unwelcome attention to their activities and inevitably make the police and media more interested in the case. William Bonin (aka The Freeway Murderer) once picked up a young man named William Pugh in his car. However, rather than kill Pugh (as Bonin usually did with any hitchhiker unlucky enough to end up in his car), Bonin let Pugh go because they had been seen together in a bar earlier. The decision not to kill Pugh though would seal Bonin's fate. In 1980, Pugh was in prison for car theft and happened to hear about the exploits of The Freeway Killer on a radio new bulletin. Pugh was pretty sure there was a good chance that this notorious Freeway Killer was William Bonin so he shared his suspicions with the authorities.

Hollywood often depicts serial killers as elusive criminal masterminds who are always two steps ahead of the police.

The reality is very different. Many serial killers are of average or below average intelligence and not exactly impossible to catch. Take Ted Bundy for example - who is often cited as being one of the most intelligent serial killers. Although a seemingly perpetual student, Ted Bundy never finished law school. Bundy was not academically gifted and this caused him great pain. When he went to college and law school he was dismayed to find that the vast majority of students were brighter than him.

It was Dennis Rader's technical incompetence and stupidity that led to his arrest. Dismayed that the BTK killer was no longer in the news, he began sending cryptic confession messages to the police and media. He ended up sending the police a floppy disk on which they retrieved deleted metadata which contained the name 'Dennis' and mentioned the local Christ Lutheran Church (where Rader was a big cheese). The police put 2 and 2 together and quickly deduced that Dennis Rader was their man. Dennis Rader liked to think of himself as a criminal genius but he was always pretty dumb. Not only did he get himself captured with his floppy disk mistake but his letters to the police and media were riddled with spelling and grammar mistakes.

A lot of serial killers are so unbalanced mentally that they leave obvious evidence. Take Richard (The Vampire of Sacramento) Chase for example. He left bloody hand and foot prints all over the place at his gory crime scenes. Arthur Shawcross was captured because he made the mistake of going back to his last crime scene - where the police were secretly waiting. Film and TV depictions of serial killers often have a trope where the killer leaves calling cards and fiendish puzzles for the police. This is largely fiction - unless one counts 'posing' bodies as a calling card. Serial killers are often completely detached from reality. This is illustrated in their frequent protestations of innocence despite indisputable evidence against them. They always seem to think their persuasive powers will somehow get them out of prison.

There are of course some exceptions to the general rule that serial killers are no more (and in many cases less) intelligent than your average 'normal' person. Jeffrey Dahmer had an IQ of 145. Edward Kemper has an IQ over 140. Rodney Alcala was found to have a very high IQ when he was tested in custody. There have been many serial killers in the medical profession. H..H Holmes went to medical school. Harold Shipman was a GP. There have been military officers exposed as serial killers. Serial killers don't really conform to any one type or group. Ultimately they are just like us and come from an eclectic range of backgrounds. Some are quite smart and some are quite dumb. Some of them are organised and some are disorganised.

One of the smartest killers was Israel Keyes - an American serial killer active from 1996 to 2012. There are three confirmed victims but the true tally is almost certainly much higher. Keyes was another serial killer with a military background. Keyes was a prolific and ruthless burglar and would kill anyone who got in his way. He raped most of his victims. He killed himself in custody in 2012 by slashing his wrists. Israel Keyes was considered to be one of the most intelligent serial killers. He would sometimes travel thousands of miles to rob and murder and planned everything out far in advance. He would hire rental cars, have a special 'murder kit' in different locations, and meticulously dispose of bodies and remains. Another smart killer was Patrick Wayne Kearney. Kearney once removed a bullet from the head of one of his victims so it could not be traced to his gun.

Studies have shown that 74% of serial killers murder their victims within a circumscribed geographic area. As a general rule (as we have just noted with Israel Keyes, there are some cunning and calculating exceptions) serial killers really don't like to travel. They tend to have a comfort zone. That comfort zone is a specific local area which they know well. Serial killers often seem to be creatures of habit. They feel more comfortable killing in an area that they have some knowledge of and are familiar with.

There was a rise in serial killers during the 1950s. Sociological theories for this include improved transport and employment (which created a more transient population where people moved around and were harder to keep track of) and the emotional fallout of the recent war. The 1970s saw a serial killer 'explosion' in America. Theories on this include mind-altering drugs and the trauma of Vietnam. It could be though that there was simply more reporting of such crimes. More news channels and live news naturally meant that serial killers got more coverage. Serial killers have always been around but in the days when there was less media their activities often tended to fly under the radar more than they would today.

Radford University's 2016 report found that 1987 was the most prolific year ever for serial killers in the United States. Serial killers were responsible for 389 deaths that year. The United States, in relation to its population, still has the most serial killers. In 2018, it was estimated that the United States had produced 2743 serial killers in its history. FBI Serial Crime Unit chief John Douglas once estimated there were around 25 to 50 active serial killers in the United States. This was felt by many to be a rather conservative estimate. While some individual serial killers are very prolific, as a general group they are not responsible for as many murders as we might think. Studies have shown that the average serial killer will kill four to five victims over an average period of six years.

In their 2016 report, Radford University found that Australia had the second highest ratio (that is to say the number of serial killers in relation to the population) of serial killers after the United States. Radford University's 2016 report also found that, among western countries with a modern media, Spain seemed to have the lowest per capita number of serial killers. In 2018, it was estimated that Canada had produced 101 serial killers in its history. In 2018, it was also estimated that England had produced 145 serial killers in its (very long) history. While we have a lot of serial killer data about western nations this is inevitably not the case though everywhere.

It is obviously rather difficult to get a completely accurate picture on serial killer statistics and details from all nations in the world. Not all countries allow unfettered reporting on serial killer cases - even to this day. In the old Soviet Union, cases of serial killers were repressed by the authorities because it reflected badly on the communist system (contrast this with the post-Soviet era - where we have many details about modern Russian and Ukrainian serial killers). It's hard to know what, for example, the true figures on serial killers are in secretive nations like China. There have cases involving serial killers in India where little is known about the killer because the authorities did not allow the trial to be covered by the media.

In the last decade there have been an estimated average of forty-three serial killers a year in the United States. Of the individual states in America, California has experienced the highest number of serial killers. Most serial killers are in their twenties or thirties. A large number of serial killers kill for the first time in their teens or twenties. The overwhelming majority of serial killers (over 80%) are white. Studies show that the overwhelming majority of serial killers are heterosexual. It won't come as a huge surprise to learn that the majority of serial killer victims are women. It is estimated that around 75% of victims are female.

Heterosexual killers nearly always kill women and gay male serial killers nearly always kill men. Nearly 20% of serial killer victims are eighteen or under. The older you are the less chance you have of being killed by a serial killer. There are exceptions of course but serial killers (when given a choice) generally tend to target very young victims.

Ted Bundy said that there were more serial killers than people think. He wasn't the first or last killer to say this. Donald Gaskins, another serial killer, said that, in his opinion, FBI estimates concerning the number of serial killers in America were far too low.

There are estimated, according to some other studies, to be as many as two thousand serial killers at large in America at any one time. That sounds rather on the high side but empirical statistics are difficult to verify for sure. The true figures for America and the world in general are impossible to say. Not all serial killers are caught. Some of them go under the radar. Sometimes serial killers even get muddled up or are the figment of contaminated DNA mistakes. The only thing we can say with some certainty is that - thankfully - there aren't nearly as many serial killers as there used to be back in the salad days of Bundy, Gacy, Ramirez, and others of an equally horrendous ilk.

What Makes Someone Become A Serial Killer And Are There Warning Signs?

We know a lot more about serial killers now than we used to do but we'll never completely understand them. We are fascinated by serial killers because they are not like us at all. Serial killers do the most appalling and gruesome things without batting an eyelid. They do things that ordinary people would never be capable of doing. Most ordinary people have compassion, guilt, empathy, and are sensitive and squeamish. We don't like blood and hate to see others in distress. These are alien emotions to serial killers when they ply their trade. They have no empathy or guilt and they love to see people in distress.

Most experts think the theory that serial killers are 'bad seeds' who were born bad is a myth. You can't be born bad. Environments and experiences turn people twisted and bad - not genetics. A large number of serial killers had unhappy childhoods. There are exceptions to this of course but many serial killers had an awful start in life. In many cases they experienced grim poverty or suffered abuse - or in many cases experienced both of these factors. It is by no means completely universal but a common thread between many serial killers often seems to be a dysfunctional relationship with their mother. It seems to a recurring pattern too that many serial killers were beaten and verbally abused by strict fathers. The 1988 publication Sexual Homicide, Patterns and Motives said that 70% of families who raised a serial killer have had a history of alcohol abuse.

There have been many cases where serial killers grew up in a house where crime was the norm. Their relatives were criminals and even their friends too. There were no role models to teach them right from wrong. The childhood of Richard (The Night Stalker) Ramirez was not exactly helped by his adoration of a cousin who served in Vietnam. This cousin filled the head of Ramirez with tales (and often photographic evidence) of war atrocities and also taught Ramirez how to use a knife. The cousin of Ramirez later shot his own wife while Ramirez was present. Arthur Shawcross (who killed fourteen people) was said to have had sexual relations with his sister. He also said his aunt and mother sexually abused him. Andrei (The Butcher of Rostov) Chikatilo grew up listening to accounts of the mass death, torture, and cannibalism in the war on the Eastern Front between the Red Army and Nazi Germany. A number of serial killers were orphaned or abandoned as children. There have been many cases of serial killers who were bullied when they were growing up.

A surprisingly high number of serial killers received head injuries from an accident in their childhood or youth. There is a theory that this impairs the part of the brain responsible for ruminating on the consequences of one's actions. 'The link between brain injury and crime is thought to be damage to the frontal lobes of the brain,' wrote the International Journal of Criminology and Sociological Theory. 'Frontal lobe injury has been associated with loss of control over sub-cortical and limbic structures involved in primitive impulses (Grafman et al, 1996). Lesions in these areas may influence functions such as social perception, self-control and judgement, as well as emotions and mood. Thus, the link between brain injury and crime may reflect the effects of brain injury-related cognitive and emotional impairments on behaviour. An individual may permissive elements of a situation, make poor social judgements, overreact to provocative stimuli, and lack the communication skills to verbally negotiate conflict or strike out impulsively.'

Richard Ramirez suffered two head injuries as a child. It is believed they left him with seizures. Nannie Doss (aka The Giggling Granny) suffered a head injury as a child when she was involved in an accident where an iron bar flew off a train and struck her. Doss tried to use this head injury as a defence for her murders. Fred West, who was one of the worst serial

killers in British history, suffered two head injuries as a
teenager when he was involved in a motorcycle crash and then
fell from a fire escape. John Wayne Gacy is another notorious
serial killer who suffered head injuries as a child. He was
knocked out by a swing and once beaten senseless by his
father. David Berkowitz (aka The Son of Sam) suffered a head
injury at the age of six when he was struck by a car. Alexander
Pichushkin (aka The Chessboard Killer) suffered a serious
head injury as a child when he was in a playground. Dennis
Rader said that when he was an infant his mother dropped
him and he landed on his head.

There are a large number of other examples of serial killers
suffering a blow to the head at a young age. Now, this
obviously does not explain all the serial killers who didn't
suffer head injuries but it certainly might have been a factor in
those who DID. Relatives of Jeffrey Dahmer say that his
personality seemed to suddenly change after he had hernia
surgery at the age of six. After this surgery, Dahmer suddenly
seemed to become a dark and aloof child. Pyromania is seen as
an early warning sign that someone has the capacity to
murder. Acts of early arson are often cited as a signal that
someone might become a serial killer. Arthur Shawcross is one
of a number of killers who liked to start fires in his youth.
David Berkowitz was also said to be obsessed with pyromania
as a child and responsible for starting many fires.

Bed wetting past the age of thirteen is sometimes cited as a
sign that someone might become a serial killer but the science
on this is debatable. A lot of serial killers seem to have had
incidents of indecent exposure at a young age. Randall
Woodfield, Ted Bundy, and Jeffrey Dahmer are examples. The
FBI once stated that, according to their research, around 70%
of serial killers have experienced drug or alcohol addictions in
their life. A large number of serial killers rely on drinks or
drugs (or both in some cases). Ted Bundy said he usually had a
drink before he murdered someone. Dennis Nilsen was a big
drinker and said that alcohol was the 'charge' and fuel for
some of his murders. A lot of seventies and eighties serial

killers like Herbert Mullin, Danny (The Gainsville Ripper) Rollings, and Richard Ramirez took industrial quantities of drugs.

Studies have indicated that serial killers do not have natural emotions like fear and anxiety. As a consequence, serial killers need to do something extreme to experience any feelings at all. Between 30% to 40% of serial killers display abnormal brainwave patterns. Abuse of animals is a common activity in many serial killers as children. Most serial killers have criminal convictions from the time before they killed. Sexual offences and robbery are the most common early offences for serial killers. Many serial killers begin their life of crime as thieves and rapists. It is often suggested in studies that the desire to kill is something that has been bubbling away beneath the surface for a while. Serial killers do not suddenly wake up one day and decide to go and kill someone. It is usually something they have thought about for a while and maybe even planned in their mind.

Studies have shown that serial killers sometimes experience hallucinations about killing prior to the stage where they actually seek out victims. These hallucinations become very vivid. It is a common trait in many serial killers to use prostitutes before they become killers. An amazingly high number of serial killers were also Peeping Toms as teenagers and young men. Ted Bundy is an obvious example of this. When he was a teenager, Bundy would roam around his neighbourhood at night trying to find windows where a woman might be undressing. A lot of these disturbed individuals seem to reach a point where their activities are not enough anymore. Peeping Tomdom is not enough. Even rape is not enough. They want to go further.

Serial killers often say that killing is very addictive once they do it for the first time. Tommy Lynn Sells was connected to around a dozen murders but he claimed to have killed about seventy people. He said that killing for him was like taking a shot of dope. It was the ultimate high and he was constantly chasing that high again once he'd sampled it. One surprisingly high factor in people becoming serial killers is pragmatism. A large number of thieves and rapists have ended up in prison for their crimes and simply deduced that the best thing to do next time around is simply kill the victims of their crimes so there won't be any witnesses to land them in prison again! An example of this would be The Acid Bath Murderer John Haigh. Haigh was a thief and fraudster who got tired of being arrested. He decided that in the future he would simply the murder the people he fleeced so that they couldn't report him.

Most serial killers develop a cold personality at a young age. They are sociopaths. Sociopaths lack a sense of responsibility or a social conscience. They are prone to antisocial behaviour. They can then tilt into becoming a psychopath. A psychopath has even less of a moral compass than a sociopath. 'Psychopathy,' wrote NCBI Resources, 'is a constellation of psychological symptoms that typically emerges early in childhood and affects all aspects of a sufferer's life including relationships with family, friends, work, and school. The symptoms of psychopathy include shallow affect, lack of empathy, guilt and remorse, irresponsibility, and impulsivity. While the typical non-psychopathic felon may ponder and struggle with life on the outside and with changing his criminal ways, the typical psychopath returns to his life of crime, and often violent and sexual crime, in the same way he does everything—impulsively, selfishly and without any regard to the rights of others, rights he does not even notice.'

Serial killers do not have a rational and logical voice in their head telling them that a course of action is wrong. They will ignore and banish any such thoughts. They have no empathy, thought, or remorse for their victims. A study by Radford University suggested that 46% of serial killers killed simply for the enjoyment. The FBI say that serial killers tend to be cautious with their first murder. They will typically choose a vulnerable person who is disconnected from conventional society - like a homeless person or sex worker. Sex workers have traditionally been a common target for serial killers.

Hitchhikers and runaways also represent 'prime' targets for serial killers. Sociological factors play a part in who some serial killers choose to kill. The American serial killer Samuel Little only killed black women because he felt they were more 'invisible' and forgotten in society than white women. Sadly, he was right about this.

Radford University's research suggested that 31% of serial killers murder for financial reasons. An example of a 'financial' serial killer would be Aileen Wuornos. She would pick up lifts from lone men in cars, make them pull over in a rural spot, and then shoot them to steal their money and valuables. Wuornos never mutilated any bodies or tortured her victims. There was no sexual enjoyment or sense of ritual to the murders. Her only concern was money. She was essentially a very ruthless and violent thief. Aileen Wuornos actually hated it when someone called her a serial killer (though she surely was - even by the broadest definition).

Some children of serial killers have expressed a fear that they might have some inherited some crazy killing gene. Fortunately, being a serial killer is not hereditary! The tension between fantasy and reality is sometimes cited as a big factor in the psychology of serial killers. Serial killers often seem detached from reality. They are overpowered by their dark fantasies and attempt to make them a part of reality. This warped conflation of fantasy and reality is present in the disturbed minds of many killers.

The strange thing about serial killers is that a number of them have a superficial charm. They can often blend into society and seem ordinary. Friends of Ted Bundy refused to believe he was a serial killer when he was initially arrested. When the horrors at 25 Cromwell Street were dug up, neighbours of Fred West were astonished to learn that their friendly neighbour was a serial killer. As Ted Bundy once said - "We serial killers are your sons, we are your husbands, we are everywhere."

How Many Serial Killers Are Cannibals?

Dr Eric Hickey, professor of forensic psychology at Walden University, estimated that around only around five to ten out of every two thousand serial killers are cannibals. It is very rare for serial killers to eat the flesh of their victims. This fact makes the known cannibal serial killers all the more infamous. There are not a huge amount of killers where we know for a fact that they ate parts of their victims and so verified killers who fall into this category are (unavoidably) all the more macabre and morbidly fascinating.

Leonarda Cianciulli was a serial killer active in Italy during World War 2. Her murders were unusual because they were motivated by a belief in black magic. Cianciulli believed that if she offered up some human sacrifices this would prevent her soldier son from coming to any harm in the war. She subsequently killed three women. The story of Leonarda Cianciulli was given a macabre gloss by what she did to her victims after she killed them. She used the blood from her victims in a recipe for tea cakes. Cianciulli also turned her last victim into bars of soap. And yes, Leonarda Cianciulli is said to have sampled the cakes she made from her unfortunate victims.

Joachim Kroll was born in Hindenburg, Upper Silesia, in 1933. Kroll killed fourteen people between 1955 and 1976. When the police entered the apartment where Kroll lived there was a hand boiling in a pan of water and human flesh in the fridge. Human waste blocked the pipes and toilet. Kroll was clearly insane. He tends to be known as The Ruhr Cannibal in true crime articles. When he was asked to explain why he had eaten parts of his victims, Kroll calmly replied that he had done this to reduce his supermarket shopping bills for food. Dorángel Vargas was known as The Hannibal Lecter of the Andes. He killed at least fourteen people in the mid 1990s in Venezuela.

Vargas was homeless and preyed on victims in a local park. He confessed to eating eleven of his victims. Vargas said he did not eat women or children because they were too pure. He also declined to eat overweight people because he said fatty flesh was less healthy.

Karl Denke was born in 1860 in the Kingdom of Prussia (now part of Poland). Denke is known as The Cannibal from Ziebice. Denke was well liked and an organist at the local Lutheran church. He had a small store which sold meat. He killed for the first time in 1903 by murdering a young slaughterhouse worker named Emma Sander (luckily for Denke, this murder was attributed to a wholly innocent man who had worked with the dead woman). The meat Denke sold in his shop was in reality the flesh of his victims. He was even a cannibal himself and sampled his own products. Denke usually pickled the meat of his victims and sold it in jars. It was clearly very popular because the shop did a flourishing trade.

Denke's gruesome exploits came to an end in 1924 when a homeless man went to the police to complain that a lunatic with an axe had just tried to murder him. When they investigated the workshop out the back of Denke's shop the police discovered that Denke had been making belts from human skin. He also used human hair to produce shoelaces. They also found huge piles of human bones and remains. These included 65 feet and metacarpal bones and 150 human ribs. There were bones from all parts of the human body and knives and axes all stained with blood. Denke was arrested but hung himself at the police station. It is believed that Denke murdered at least forty people to provide meat for his shop. Because there was no trial or police interview, Denke never explained what exactly had made him sell human flesh in his shop and kill all those people.

Nikolai Espolovich Dzhumagaliev was a Soviet serial killer who was convicted of seven murders committed from 1979 to 1980. He is known as Kolya the Maneater because he ate the flesh of some of his victims. Of his first murder, Dzhumagaliev told the police - "I cut the corpse's breast into strips, removed the ovaries, and separated the pelvis and hips; I then put these pieces into a backpack and carried them home. I melted the fat to fry with, and some parts I pickled. Once, I put the parts through a meat grinder and made dumplings. I saved the meat for myself; I never served it to anyone else. Twice, I grilled parts—the heart and the kidneys. Grilled meat, too. But it was tough, and I had to cook it for a long time in its own fat. The meat of this woman took me a month to eat. The first time I ate human flesh, I had to force myself, but then I got used to it."

Albert Fish was born in Washington, D.C. in 1870. He molested over 400 children and tortured and killed an unverified number of others. We will never know exactly how many people Fish might have killed. Fish is an infamous bogeyman in true crime lore and always claimed to be a cannibal. The flesh from one of the legs of one of the child victims of Fish had been hacked away. He once told the police that he made a stew out of the nose and ears of one of his victims. No wonder Albert Fish is considered to have been one of the inspirations for Hannibal Lecter. The most infamous crime of Fish came when he pretended to be hiring farm workers and met the Budd family (whose father Edward was seeking employment). Fish persuaded them to let their ten year-old daughter Grace visit him to attend a birthday party for his niece but - of course - it was all a ruse and Grace turned up to find Fish alone. Fish later sent the Budd family a letter in which he claimed to have cooked and eaten Grace after he killed her.

Özgür Dengiz was a Turkish killer who killed two people and attempted to kill another. His crimes took place from 1997 to 2007. When he was captured, Dengiz was found to have human flesh in his fridge. Dengiz said he liked human flesh so much he would even eat it raw. Peter Bryan was a killer who murdered three people in England from 1993 to 2004.

When he was captured by the police in 2004, Bryan was

cooking parts of a victim's brain in a frying pan. "I ate his brains with butter," Bryan told the police. "It was really nice." Bryan was completely insane. He was sent to Broadmoor Hospital - where he later killed another inmate because he said he wanted to eat more human flesh.

Zhang Yongming was a Chinese serial killer responsible for at least eleven murders from 2008 to 2012. He sold the flesh of his victims at a local market and pretended it was ostrich meat. When he was arrested, the police found that Yongming had preserved human eyeballs in jars. The flesh of his victims was hanging up to dry. Alexander Bychkov was a Russian serial killer who killed nine men from 2009 to 2012. In his confession to the police, Bychkov claimed that he ate livers, hearts and the muscle of his victims.

Fritz Haarmann, a German serial Killer most active in the early decades of the 20th century, was known as The Vampire of Hanover because he would bite the necks of his victims.

Fritz Haarmann is believed to have killed twenty-seven people. He dumped the remains in the Leine River. The police found 500 human bones in this river. Haarmann sold meat on the black market. You can probably guess what type of meat he is speculated to have used. Richard Chase was born in Santa Clara, California, in 1950. Chase was later nicknamed The Vampire of Sacramento when he achieved infamy as a deranged serial killer. He picked up this grisly and theatrical moniker because he liked to drink the blood of animals and his human victims. When the police searched the apartment of Chase they found traces of blood everywhere - including the kitchen utensils.

Vladimir Nikolayev was sentenced to death in 1997 for killing and cannibalizing two people in the town of Novocheboksary in Russia. Nikolayev told investigators - "I was coming home from a party a little drunk and next to the door of my building there was another guy; also drunk who asked me for a light. We started arguing and it got into a fight. He hit me and I hit

him and it turned out he died. What was I to do? I dragged
him to the bathroom, undressed him and started cutting him
apart. I cut off his head, arms, legs and all of a sudden
something kinda struck me and I thought I would try him. I
cut off a piece of meat from his thigh and boiled it. I tried it,
but didn't like it so I chopped it up and fried it in a frying pan.
I gave the meat to one of my friends, he took it home - gave it
to his wife. She made dumplings with it, had some herself and
fed it to her children. Well, I said it was kangaroo. We don't
have kangaroos around here. They didn't know what it was."

Alferd Packer was known as The Colorado Cannibal. He was a
prospector and murderer who ate human flesh to survive in
the wilderness in 1874. He was later captured and imprisoned.
'Like thousands of other men of his time,' wrote
coloradovirtuallibrary.org, 'Alferd (sometimes spelled Alfred)
Packer caught gold fever and sought to make his fortune in the
mountains of Colorado. During the winter of 1873-74, Packer
joined a group of five other men, whose names were Shannon
Bell, James Humphrey, Frank Miller, George Noon, and Israel
Swan. The men had met Chief Ouray, who told them to
postpone their journey until spring, but the men ignored the
Chief's advice. In February, the six men ran out of food. Alone
in the wilderness and trapped in heavy snows, the men soon
resorted to boiling their moccasins for food. After a few days,
even that ran out. According to Packer, the men became so
hungry that one night, Bell came after Packer with a hatchet.
Packer turned on Bell and killed him. Packer claimed that he
then found the bodies of his other companions and that the
flesh had been torn from one of them. That is when, Packer
said, he was forced to eat the meat of the other men, or
otherwise starve to death.'

Yoo Young-chul is a South Korean serial killer who claimed to
have eaten the flesh of his victims. He was active between
2003 and 2004 and claimed to have killed twenty people.
Many of his victims were prostitutes who he bludgeoned to
death. He also killed a number of rich men. Yoo Young-chul
said that his motivation for killing was bitterness at the

poverty he had grown up in. He didn't think it was fair that some people had more money than they could ever spend while others had to live in squalor. His capture ignited a debate in South Korea over whether the death penalty should be used. The country has not executed anyone since 1997. In the end, Yoo Young-chul was not executed and still resides in prison.

In 1830, a criminal named Edward Broughton was transported from England to Tasmania (then known as Van Diemen's Land) in Australia to work in a penal colony. Broughton ended up on a work party of five convicts. There was only one police constable in charge of the party and the prisoners attacked him and escaped. The men had an axe (which they had stolen from their work party) and trekked through the wilderness in search of food. They were eventually exhausted and starving. Broughton decided they would simply have to eat one of the convicts. As a consequence, Richard Hutchinson (who was convicted for horse theft) was murdered by Broughton with the axe and his body was roasted over a fire. Broughton made a pact with a teenage convict in the party named Patrick Fagan. They both watched over one another while the other was asleep. Broughton kept a firm grip on the precious axe. The axe gave him power over the group.

William Coventry, the oldest of the convicts, was chosen to be the next victim when they ran out of food again. He was killed with the axe and his flesh roasted over another fire. The men ate as much as they could and then stuffed the remaining human flesh in their pockets for later. The convicts continued their trek and thoughts turned to who would be next to eat. Broughton was asked to kill Fagan but he refused to allow the death his friend. The matter was taken out of his own hands though when one of the remaining convicts named Matthew Macavoy murdered Fagan with the axe when Broughton was asleep. Broughton and Macavoy cooked the body and had a large meal. Broughton and Macavoy gave themselves up a few days later when they reached an outpost. In 1832 they were hung for murder and cannibalism. Broughton made a full confession.

'The first man we murdered was Hutchinson,' wrote
Broughton. 'We were nearly starving at the time, and we drew
lots who should kill him; Hutchinson was asleep: the lot fell
upon me, and I killed him with an axe, which we brought with
us. He was cut to pieces, and with the exception of the
intestines, hands, feet and head, the body was carried with us.
We lived somedays on his flesh; we ate it heartily- I do not
know how many days it lasted. After having thus committed
murder, we began to be afraid of each other; one night I awoke
Fagan, and told him to watch while I slept, and I would watch
while he slept, for I feared that I should be murdered; we each
of us feared, that on going to sleep we should be dispatched by
the others. One night, as Coventry was cutting wood, we other
three agreed to kill him; he was an old man of nearly sixty. I
refused to do it as I said they ought to kill him among them, so
we might all be in the same trouble.

'Fagan struck the old man the first blow with the axe; Coventry
saw him coming, and cried out for mercy; he struck him just
above the eye, but did not kill him - Macavoy and myself
finished him and cut him in pieces. We lived upon his body for
some days; we were not starving when we killed Coventry' we
had only consumed the remains of Hutchinson the same day.
We were not at all sparring of the food we obtained from the
bodies of our companions: we eat it as if we had abundance-if
we had been sparing of it, the one would have been sufficient
for us. We now became daily more afraid of each other. Before
we had consumed Coventry's body, Macavoy one night started
up from the fire, and asked me to go down with him into the
bush to see if we could find a kangaroo track, that we might set
a snare for. When leaving the fire, Macavoy said, "Bring the
axe with you." When we had gone about 300 yards, Macavoy
laid down and asked me to stop and sit down. I was afraid; I
thought he wanted to take away my life, and he was stronger
than me. I then threw the axe further from him than from
myself, so that if he attempted to take it, I thought I could get
it before him.

'He did not offer to touch it, he then said, "there are three of us, Fagan is young and foolish, people will frighten him; and he will tell what has been done, now the only thing that we can do to pre- vent it is to kill him."' I said l would not agree to it, that I knew him better than he did, and was acquainted with his ways and that he would not tell. I could trust my life in his hands. Macavoy said that he was sure he would tell, he would be frightened, as there was three of us, he would turn evidence as to these murders, to save his own life, and we should be hanged ; when there are only you and I together, we could not turn evidence against each other, we can say that we left them at Gordon's River, at the back of the Frenchman's Cap, because they could not swim over it, and then it would be supposed that they had lost themselves and perished in the bush, and then we should perhaps be sent to Norfolk Island. I replied that Fagan was a very good swimmer, and that he was known to be so as well as myself, and they would also know that I would not go away and leave him.

'We then returned to the fire and agreed not to kill him. When we went back he was lying down by the fire, his shoes were off, and his feet were towards the fire, he was warming them. I then threw the axe down, and he looked up and said, have you put any snares down Ned? I said no, I have not put any down, there are snares enough if you but know it. I sat by him; Macavoy sat beyond me, he was on my right hand, and Fagan on my left. I was wishing to tell Fagan what had passed, but could not, as Macavoy was sitting with the axe close to him, looking at us. Then I lay down, and was in a doze, when I heard Fagan scream out; i leaped up on my feet in a dreadful fright and saw Fagan lying on his back with a dreadful cut in his head, and the blood pouring from it; Macavoy was standing over him with the axe in his hand. I cried to Macavoy you murdering rascal, you blood-thirsty wretch, what have you done? He said this will save our lives, and then he struck him another blow on the head with the axe. Fagan then groaned, and Macavoy cut his throat with a razor through the windpipe.

'We then began to strip Fagin, we stripped him naked. Fagan had on a red shirt, which I had stolen from Bradshaw at the Settlement, and which occasioned words and ill-feeling between Macavoy and myself, as to whom should become possessed of it; Fagan had also a red comforter and cap, which I likewise stole from Bradshaw, and gave him. I robbed Bradshaw of all I could lay my hands on, I left him not a mouthful of food when I came away. Bradshaw had always been very kind to me, and gave me anything in his power: But I have endeavoured to kill him by making a tree fall upon him on account of his being a Constable, and getting people flogged. Fagan's body we cut up into pieces, and roasted it; we roasted all but the hands, feet, and head; we roasted all at once, upon all occasions, as it was lighter to carry, and would keep longer, and not be so easily discovered. About two days after Fagan's murder, we heard some dogs, they had caught a kangaroo, and the dogs were wild. We got the kangaroo, and threw away the remainder of the body. Two days after this we gave ourselves up. I wish this statement to be made public after my death that it may serve as a warning.'

The most famous cannibal killer is of course Jeffrey Dahmer. Dahmer was convicted on 15 counts of first-degree murder. Dahmer fried the body parts of his victims in a skillet before he ate them. Dahmer used a meat tenderizer to make human flesh more tender and edible. During his police confession, Jeffrey Dahmer was asked if he ate human body parts plain. He replied that he ate them with salt & pepper and steak sauce. Dahmer had a special tray at the bottom of his fridge to collect the blood that dripped down from body parts. Jeffrey Dahmer would sometimes make sandwiches for neighbours in his apartment building. It is therefore highly possible that his neighbours might have unwittingly eaten human flesh. Dahmer had a very (what else?) deadpan sense of humour. He would tell journalists in prison that human biceps tasted like a good cut of steak. Dahmer tends to be known as The Milwaukee Cannibal in true crime circles today. Dahmer said he ate parts of his victims because he wanted them to always be a part of him.

Why Do Many Serial Killers Seem To Be Into Necrophilia?

Necrophilia is not uncommon amongst the most notorious serial killers. Ownership and total control of a person is a common fantasy that fuels the depraved activities of the worst serial killers. It is a popular thread with many serial killers that their sexual fantasies from a young age were about people who are restrained or can't move or struggle. Social scientists say that the desire for control and dominance we see in serial killers often stems from an unhappy childhood where they felt weak and vulnerable. Many serial killers love the thought of having a helpless sexual victim at their mercy and you don't get more helpless than being dead. Studies have shown that necrophilic serial killers are much more likely to mutilate and cut up the victims. A study once found that 86% of serial killers had violent sexual fantasies that involved mutilation and restrained victims. Lester and White found that 100% of the serial killer necrophiles in their study were male. This is generally not something that female serial killers (female serial killers do exist) indulge in.

'Necrophilia,' wrote sciencedirect.com, 'is a term derived from the Greek words philios (attraction to/love) and nekros (dead body) and involves the sexual attraction to a dead body. Surprisingly, necrophilia dates back hundreds of years and has been documented in Greek mythology, ancient cultures, the Greco-Roman period, the middle ages, and in the modern era. Mortuary attendants and funeral home workers have been known to be caught sexually assaulting corpses, and there have been individuals who have dug up graves in order to obtain a dead body to have sex with. More commonly there are serial murderers such as Ed Gein, Ed Kemper, Jeffrey Dahmer, and Garry Ridgeway who have taken sexual advantage of dead victims.' Necrophilia is a common postmortem activity for sexual serial killers because it doesn't give the victim the opportunity reject the offender.

Gary Ridgway was born in 1949 in Salt Lake City, Utah. He is known as The Green River Killer and was convicted of 49 murders. The true kill count is almost certainly a lot higher than that figure. Ridgway, like many serial killers, targeted sex workers and teenage runaways and hitchhikers. Ridgway would usually strangle the victims and then sexually abuse the bodies - which he would leave in the woods and return to again. Gary Ridgway said he sometimes tried to bury victims as soon as he could because otherwise he was tormented by an insatiable urge to have sex with the corpses. Ted Bundy (by now captured) was consulted by the police when they were trying to solve the Green River Killer case. Bundy told the police that the killer probably returned to burial sites to visit the bodies of his victims. He was certainly right about that.

Jerry Brudos was a serial killer who murdered four women in Oregon from 1968 to 1969. Brudos was a rapist and necrophile who killed because he couldn't control his foot fetish. He sawed off the foot of one victim and put in the freezer. He would then often take the foot out of the freezer and put ladies shoes on it. Jerry Brudos cut off the breasts of one of his victims so he could make plastic moulds with it. Jerry Brudos actually got married. It was said that he liked his wife to do the housework naked wearing nothing but a pair of high heeled shoes. Jerry Brudos was thankfully captured quite quickly. He died in prison in 2006. His prison cell was said to be full of ladies shoe catalogues when he died.

Jane Toppan, who was born in Boston, was a famous serial killer who entered medical school in 1885. She murdered 31 people with lethal injections in her duties as a nurse. She was known as The Angel of Death. Toppan was jilted at the alter. This is speculated to have been one of the sources of her anger and mental health problems. Toppan first attracted suspicion in her medical duties because she was completely obsessed with autopsies. Toppan absolutely loved visiting the morgue. She was known as Jolly Jane to her colleagues because she was always laughing and smiling. Toppan was brought to justice in

1901 after killing an entire family. Toppan is said to have got a
sexual thrill from her murders. She said she climbed into bed
with patients she had killed. Toppan was sent to a mental
institution and died in 1938.

The notorious graverobber Ed Gein was born in La Crosse
County, Wisconsin, on August 27, 1906. He is not generally
felt (in terms of statistics) to be a serial killer but he might well
have been. Gein probably killed more people than he is
officially credited with. Gein had an isolated life on the family
farm but his mental health eroded after the death of his
mother and brother. Gein's brother died in a mysterious
accident involving fires on the farm. Many suspect Ed Gein of
killing his brother. Ed Gein never got over the death of his
mother. He was a childlike man who was fond of lurid
paperbacks and comics that featured stories about cannibals
and Nazis. In 1957, Plainfield hardware store owner Bernice
Worden vanished. The police deduced from cash register
receipts that Ed Gein had been one of the last visitors to the
store so they went to his farm. At the farm they found the body
of Worden decapitated and hung up like a deer. It turned out
too that Ed Gein had been digging up bodies from the local
cemetery and making masks, furniture, and skin suits from
them.

At Gein's farm, the police also found the head of a woman
named Mary Hogan who had been missing for three years.
Gein used female genitalia in some of the bric-a-brac around
his home. He'd also fashioned some skulls into serving bowls.
When the police searched Ed Gein's house they found his
kitchen full of maggots. They could not fathom how anyone
could live in such squalor. The police found one room in Gein's
farmhouse untouched and free of ghoulish graveyard bric-a-
brac. His mother's bedroom - save for dust - was exactly how
she had left it when she died. You might say this was pure
Norman Bates. Gein was one of the first killers to gain national
attention in America. His crimes were so bizarre that a morbid
fascination with the case was unavoidable. Gein was arrested
and sent to a prison hospital. Ed Gein's farm burned down

after his arrest (it was said to be accident but you never know). The locals were very happy when this happened because they didn't want the farm to attract curious sightseers.

Patrick Wayne Kearney was born in East Los Angeles in 1939. He confessed to 35 murders but the true figure is most likely considerably higher. Kearney is sometimes known as The Trash Bag Killer in true crime biographies. This is because he would dismember his victims into trash bags and dump them by the side of the road or put them in the desert. He was not only a killer but a necrophile too. Kearney spent most of his spare time trawling the underbelly of the gay scene. His victims were mostly young men but he killed boys too. Kearney was only 5'5 tall and not the most physically imposing man. For this reason he used a gun and would shoot his victims dead while they were asleep or sitting in the car passenger seat next to him. He would then drive to a secluded spot and sexually abuse the body. Kearney said he would sometimes punch and kick the bodies of dead victims because he found this cathartic.

Thor Nis Christiansen was a Danish-American killer who murdered four young women in California from 1976 to 1979. Christiansen was also a necrophile. In fact, this is what had motivated the murders in the first place. He had been overwhelmed by dark fantasies of shooting a woman dead and then having sex with the body. John Christie was born in Yorkshire in 1899. Christie murdered at least eight people in London in the 1940s and 1950s - mostly by use of domestic gas. Once they were unconscious he would rape and then murder the victims. Christie is arguably not strictly a necrophile but he was close enough. He liked his victims to be inert and lifeless before he raped them. Dead or unconscious - it made no difference to Christie.

Earle Nelson was born in 1897 in San Francisco, California. He tends to be known as The Dark Strangler. Earle was the first prolific American serial killer of the 20th century (indeed for many years he thought to be the MOST prolific American serial killer - at least until the serial killer explosion of later years). Nelson's killing spree began in 1926. His modus operandi soon became clear. Nelson would dress him quite smartly and, Bible in hand, pretend to be a Christian traveller looking for a room to rent. His targets were middle-aged landladies. Once he had charmed the landlady sufficiently and got his foot inside the door (so to speak), Nelson would strangle them (sometimes with a chord) and then usually have sex with the body. He was - of course - a necrophile in addition to being a serial killer. He is credited with 22 murders but there are at least seven unsolved murders where he is considered to be a suspect.

'Some people who work in the medical and funeral industries get so used to death and bodies that becoming attracted to one takes fewer cognitive leaps,' wrote the Crime Library.

'It happened in 1931 in Key West, Florida. Radiologist Carl von Cosel, 56, became obsessed with one of the tuberculosis patients at the sanatorium where he worked. Her name was Maria Elena de Hoyos and she was a beautiful, 22-year-old woman. Von Cosel hoped to marry her, but before she could respond to his attentions, she weakened and died. He begged the family not to bury her. Fearing contamination of her body from groundwater, he built a mausoleum for her in the nearby cemetery and preserved her in formaldehyde. There in secret he would sit and have conversations with her.

'He even left a phone in the mausoleum so he could speak to her while away. This man was clearly obsessed. One day he just decided to illegally remove her corpse and take her to his home. To keep her in good shape, von Cosel brought in a regular supply of preservatives and perfumes, but Maria Elena's corpse eventually began to deteriorate. Using piano wire to string her bones together, von Cosel replaced her rotted eyes with glass eyes and her decomposed skin with a mixture of wax and silk. As her hair fell out, he used it to make a wig to put on her head. Stuffing her corpse with rags to keep her from collapsing and dressing her in a bridal gown, he kept her by his side in bed. Dr. Michael Baden pointed out on HBO's Autopsy that the man even inserted a tube into her decrepit corpse to serve as a vagina for making love. He also played a small organ to her as she slept.

'He got away with this for seven years until de Hoyos' sister accidentally came upon her in von Cosel's home. Horrified, she called the police. Von Cosel was arrested, but the statute of limitations had run out on his crime of grave robbing, so he was set free. Maria Elena was buried in a secret unmarked area and von Cosel moved to central Florida, where he sold postcards of his beloved. Even when she was taken from him, he couldn't forget her. When he eventually died in 1952, he was found in a room with a large doll in his arms that was wearing Elena's death mask.'

Yoshio Kodaira was a Japanese serial killer who raped and murdered at least seven women from 1945 to 1946. Kodaira would lure the victims to rural spots under the guise of offering them employment. He was found to have a particular fondness for having sex with the victims after he had killed them. Reginald Oates is an American killer who killed four young boys within the span of two days in April 1968, in Baltimore, Maryland. Oates had sex with the bodies of the victims after their death. When he was captured he had body parts (including genitals) from the murdered victims in a bag. Oates was deemed too insane to stand trial and sent to the Clifton T. Perkins State Hospital in Jessup.

Serhiy Tkach was born in Russia in 1952. He tends to be known as The Pavlohrad Maniac. There are 37 confirmed victims of Tkach but he claims to have killed a hundred people. Believe it or not, Serhiy Tkach worked as a criminal investigator. Tkach targeted young girls (none older than eighteen) who he then raped and suffocated. There is evidence that Tkach was a necrophile as some of the victims were apparently sexually abused after death. Ted Bundy said that after he killed a woman, he would sometimes shampoo their hair so they had less of an odour. Bundy would have sex with the bodies until decomposition made this impossible. The victims were usually stored in the woods so that Bundy could go back and visit them.

Tsutomu Miyazaki was a killer active in the late eighties and early nineties. He has been described as the Japanese version of Albert Fish. His victims were all very young children (always female) and he would post the remains to the relatives as a means of taunting them. Miyazaki was fond of necrophilia and also once returned to one of the bodies weeks after the murder to cut off the feet. Tsutomu Miyazaki was captured when he tried to abduct two girls but was noticed and had to flee. The police arrived quickly enough to capture him before he could hide or get out of the area. Miyazaki was executed by hanging in 2008. The case of Tsutomu Miyazaki was very traumatic for the people of Japan.

'Necrophiles,' wrote psychologytoday, 'have increased likelihood to commit homicide before carrying out necrophilic acts, simply because diminished empathy and antisocial behaviour are characteristic of these disorders. There has also been suggestion that those who have committed necrophilia have suffered from depression and schizophrenia in the form of anthropophagy and vampirism. The need for an unrejecting partner is universal for most humans who desire an intimate relationship with another living human, as is the need to feel accepted. And so with necrophilia, it would be worth assessing all of the qualities people look for in a living person (using dating websites, and the ample pop psychology outlets), and seeing if those needs could be met with a deceased partner. A dead partner is not judgemental, there is no fear of needing to produce a reciprocal orgasm during sex, they cannot emotionally hurt anyone, they can be trusted, they do not answer back, there is no concern about offspring, and they can meet what is only a temporary need for sexual intimacy. The necrophiliac also has the luxury of creating, imagining, or fantasizing the corpse to be anything they want it to be.'

The British serial Killer Dennis Nilsen briefly served in the

police as a younger man. When he was in the police, Nilsen
had to view autopsied bodies in the morgue. He found this
experience completely fascinating and sexually exciting.
Nilsen's passion for necrophilia was the main motive for his
murders. By the time he reached his late twenties, Nilsen was
aware that he found dead people more attractive than living
ones. Dennis Nilsen had an obsession (a fetish one might say)
with death. He saw a beautiful serenity and peace in death.
This stemmed from a childhood experience when he saw his
dead grandfather. Nilsen said that looking at dead people also
made him feel invulnerable. Dennis Nilsen liked to sleep next
to the bodies of his victims. Nilsen said he enjoyed caring for
the corpses of his victims and liked to dress them up.

As a young man, Dennis Nilsen would smear himself with
white makeup and pretend he was dead. He said he found this
erotic. Nilsen confessed that he did sexually abuse the dead
bodies of his victims but said it was non-penetrative. Nilsen
would sometimes position the body of a victim next to him and
watch television with them. Dennis Nilsen's first victim was
Stephen Holmes. Stephen went missing in December 1978 and
was only fourteen years-old. Stephen Holmes spent the night
with Dennis Nilsen. Nilsen didn't want Stephen Holmes to
leave and so strangled and drowned him. He washed the body
(including the hair) and abused the corpse sexually. Dennis
Nilsen, like Jeffrey Dahmer, didn't want people to ever leave
him - even if it meant he had to kill them. The corpse would
become like a possession or toy for Nilsen. He would derive a
bizarre sense of comfort from having a dead body to talk to or
sit with.

Psychopaths in Life wrote of Dennis Nilsen - 'It is this
tendency for people to leave him, combined with a
psychopathic desire on his part for power and control over
others, that led to him preventing some guests from leaving by
killing them and keeping their corpses. He would then keep
the corpses in his flat, often for days, sometimes even
conversing with them as if they were still alive. This
represented an extreme and perverted need for control over

others which is prevalent in all psychopaths to some degree. If
he couldn't make them stay with him voluntarily, it is as if he
would force them to stay with him by murdering them.
However despite this need for control, his lack of emotional
connection with his victims is apparent in the way he treated
their bodies when he wanted rid of them, cutting them up like
peaces of meat and keeping them in his apartment or else
burying them in his garden. Once he no longer needed them
them they were nothing to him, just objects to be disposed of.'

What Are The Most Gruesome And Strange Signatures Of Serial Killers?

A number of serial killers leave the bodies of victims in shocking or strange poses for the police or public to find. This would appear to be a case of the killer enjoying the dominance and control they have exerted over a victim. Serial killers seem to enjoy the thought of leaving a 'shocking' crime scene for the relatives and authorities to discover. Serial killers nearly always keep souvenirs from their crimes. Dahmer kept body parts, Bundy kept polaroids, and Joel Rifkin kept jewelry. Dennis Radar was was found to have a collection of driving licences belonging to his victims. It's very common for serial killers to take 'trinkets' from their victims as a keepsake. It can be something innocuous like a driving licence or rings or - in more grisly fashion - can be body parts.

Joel Rifkin was a Long Island based serial killer who was convicted in 1993 for nine murders. Rifkin targeted sex workers and was especially gruesome in the fashion in which he left his victims. He once left the decapitated head of one victim on a golf course. Rifkin clearly got off on the thought of someone discovering this gruesome display he had left in a public place. Fred West had a strange habit of removing the toes and fingers of his victims. Gary Ridgway liked to cut off the fingernails of his victims. Ted Bundy had a custom of killing in the headlights of his car or during a full moon. Bundy liked to see exactly what he was doing.

When he was captured, Jeffrey Dahmer told the police that he retained the skulls and bones of his victims because he wanted to use them to construct a place of meditation. Dahmer had spray painted the skulls because he thought this made them look more like movie props and would make them less suspicious if anyone found them. The fact that he had numerous other body parts in his apartment surely wouldn't have helped though! Edward Kemper cut out the tongue and larynx of his mother and put it in the waste disposal. He also used his mother's decapitated head as a dartboard. Kemper said that whenever he saw a pretty girl one part of him wanted to go on a date with her and the other part of him wondered what her head would look like on a stick.

Nannie Doss was especially fond of murdering her husbands. Rat poison was her preferred method of murder. She would put the poison in plum cakes. David Parker Ray was an American killer and rapist who turned his motor home into a torture dungeon. When he was apprehended in 1999 he was dubbed The Toy-Box Killer. David Parker Ray held women hostage in his 'dungeon truck' as sex slaves. They were greeted with a terrifying audio message from Ray in which he explained how hopeless their situation now was. It is not known how many people he might have killed. He died of a heart-attack only a year into his sentence. David Parker Ray was said to have spent $100,000 turning his motor home into a torture dungeon.

Sean Vincent Gillis is a serial killer who raped, murdered, and mutilated eight women in the Baton Rouge area between 1994 and 2004. Gillis, who got good grades at school and looked quite meek and placid in person, was an example of not judging a book by its cover. Gillis kept body parts as mementos and had nearly 50 photographs of his victims on his computer when he was captured. Serial killers taking photographs of their victims is fairly common. Robert Hansen was a killer most active in the 1970s. He moved to Alaska where he opened a bakery. However, he had a very disturbing and sadistic hobby. Hansen would kidnap women (many of whom were prostitutes or dancers from strip clubs) and then turn them loose in the wilderness so he could hunt them. He eventually confessed to thirteen murders.

Albert Fish had a number of strange and disturbing signatures. He would leave some of his child victims hanging from trees. William Bonin - aka The Freeway Killer - was known to use an icepick to murder people. One of the signature methods of the very violent Yorkshire Ripper was to hit women with a hammer. Jeffrey Dahmer drilled a hole in the head of some of his victims and poured in hydrochloric acid in an attempt to create a 'living' zombie. Jeffrey Dahmer would sedate his victims by giving them a drink that was laced with sleeping pills. In January 1978, Ted Bundy broke into a dorm at Florida State University and attacked four students. One was throttled with a nylon stocking and another was found dead with her nipple bitten off. Another victim suffered a broken jaw. Bundy left but then attacked a woman several streets away so brutally she was left with a fractured skull.

Lawrence Sigmund Bittaker and Roy Lewis Norris became known as The Tool Box Killers after raping and killing five teenage women in California in 1979. They lured the women to a van where they would then rape and torture the victims before killing them. This is generally regarded to be perhaps the most disturbing true crime case ever because of the harrowing nature of the torture these awful men inflicted on their victims. The screams and pleas of mercy by one victim were recorded by the men and later played at the trial. Prosecutors and members of the jury were reduced to tears at this recording and people fled the public gallery in distress. Lawrence Bittaker, who smirked throughout the trial, was described by the FBI as the coldest and most evil man they had ever interviewed. The killers stood trial in 1980 and both died in prison decades later.

Danny (The Gainsville Ripper) Rolling's worst crimes took place when he moved to Florida. In 1990 he forced his way into the home of two University of Florida students and raped and killed them. He abused the victims sexually when they were dead and cut off one of the student's nipples. The next day he forced his way into the apartment of another teenager and raped and killed her. He decapitated the victim and left the head next to some books. Rolling then killed two more students in the same month in equally grisly fashion. One was murdered in her bed. Rolling, like a number of other killers, liked to leave the bodies of female victims in sexually explicit poses.

Patrick David Mackay murdered eleven people in England from 1974 to 1975. Mackay, who was from Kent, was disturbed from a young age and once tried to set a church on fire. Mackay somehow befriended a priest named Father Anthony Crean. Crean tried to help Mackay (even when Mackay stole from him) but Mackay eventually killed the priest with an axe.

Mackay killed another man with an axe and his awful catalogue of crimes included throwing a woman from a train and kicking a homeless man off a bridge. Mackay was so devoid of humanity he once killed a 92 year-old woman with his bare hands. Due to diminished responsibility (Mackay was clearly insane), Patrick David Mackay was convicted of manslaughter and given life in prison in 1975.

Richard (The Vampire of Sacramento) Chase entered the house of a woman who was pregnant and shot her. He indulged in necrophilia with the body and then used a knife to remove some of her internal organs. Chase then drank some of the blood of the victim and stuffed dog faeces in her mouth. Luis Garavito was a Columbian serial killer who targeted orphans and runaways. He would pose as a farmer looking for workers. One of the methods of murder he employed was to use a screwdriver. Dennis Rader would sometimes take bodies of his victims to the local Christ Lutheran Church to photograph them in bondage poses. Jack the Ripper was responsible for some very grisly crime scenes. The Ripper even removed the intestines of a victim.

Béla Kiss was a Hungarian serial killer who killed over twenty women from 1900 to 1914. The bodies were found in huge drums and had been pickled. They also had puncture wounds in their necks. Kiss was never found because he was conscripted in World War I and then vanished. John Wayne Gacy, who killed over thirty young men, would sometimes contact the police and report one of the men he had killed as missing. This was a tactic designed to make him seem trustworthy and throw the police off his scent. One of John Wayne Gacy's methods of getting his victims handcuffed was to pretend he was demonstrating a magic trick. He would escape from the handcuffs himself and then challenge the victim to do the same. Gacy would usually try and get his victims a bit drunk for this game. By the time they realised it was not a game and that Gacy was dangerous it was all too late. They were already helpless.

Gordon Frederick Cummins was a killer who became known as The Blackout Ripper for murdering four women during the German bombing raids on London in World War 2. Cummins, who was in the Royal Air Force, was a very sick and savage killer. He slashed one woman's throat with a can opener and would sexually mutilate the victims. Cummins was hanged in Wandsworth Prison in 1942. The crimes of the 'Blackout Ripper' during World War 2 were suppressed by the authorities because Londoners already had enough to worry about with the Luftwaffe bombing them. They didn't need a serial killer panic thrown in too.

If the Golden State Killer Joseph James DeAngelo encountered a male in a house he was robbing, raping, and murdering in, he was said to tie the male up and balance plates on him. He would tell the male that if he heard a single sound he would kill him. DeAngelo would sometimes telephone women he had raped simply to taunt them. DeAngelo would break into the houses of his victims before his ACTUAL break-in to take ammunition out of guns and hide any potential weapons. He wanted to make his victims as vulnerable as possible.

Leonard Lake and Charles Ng were a notorious serial killing duo who abducted, raped and tortured from 1983 to 1985. Lake was the boss of the duo and although Ng was much younger he was no less sadistic. These two evil men were both crazy. They had a military background and were into survivalist conspiracy theories. They might have killed 30 people although the verifiable figure is around twelve. They built a special bunker to keep their victims captive as sex slaves.

Some of Andrei Chikatilo's victims were missing their uterus and nipples when discovered. Peter Kürten is usually known as The Vampire of Dusseldorf. His main killing spree began in 1929. Kürten was a very brutal and sadistic killer. He targeted people regardless of age and would often frenziedly stab them dozens of times with scissors. He would sexually abuse dead bodies and found this very exciting. Kürten loved the thought that his murders were attracting attention. He found it a great thrill to think that he was shocking and disgusting people. He even tried to nail one victim to a tree for the police to find but couldn't lift her because she was too heavy. In addition to stabbings, he often attacked victims with a hammer.

Robert Berdella was a serial killer who restrained, tortured, and killed at least six men from 1984 to 1987 in Kansas City, Missouri. He was known as The Kansas City Butcher. His victims were all young men that he had gained the trust of and then isolated. The murders were very sadistic - even for a serial killer. Berdella would drug and restrain the victims and then basically torture them for as long as they could survive. The victims were raped, cut, given electric shocks, and he would even inject them with cleaning fluids in the neck so they couldn't scream. Berdella would often the break the bones of the victims' hands with an iron bar so that they couldn't put up a struggle. Robert Berdella ran a booth at a market called Bob's Bizarre Bizarre which sold oddities and antiques. It is sometimes suggested that he might sold some of the skulls of his victims at this booth.

Lorenzo Gilyard is usually known as The Kansas City Strangler. He raped and murdered thirteen girls and women and is still suspected of other murders. Gilyard's signature was to stuff cloth or paper towels in the mouths of his victims. Most of them were found with their mouths stuffed like this. Gilyard sometimes left the bodies in strange explicit poses and quite often their hands were tightly bound. David Berkowitz became known as Son of Sam. He was a killer who launched random attacks in New York in 1976 and 1977. There were six confirmed victims. Berkowitz claimed that the dog of a neighbour was possessed by a spirit that had ordered him to kill. Berkowitz knew how to use a gun from his time in the army. He would approach people in cars and on the street and then shoot them with no warning. Some of these people survived - but were left with terrible injuries.

Harvey Glatman was a killer active in the 1950s. He is believed to have killed four women. He would pretend to be a photographer to lure victims and was dubbed The Lonely Hearts Killer because he also lured a victim with a lonely hearts ad in the newspaper. Glatman would rape and murder the victims. When he was caught, the police found a toolbox that Glatman used to store disturbing photographs of his bound victims. Glatman was given the death sentence and killed in the gas chamber of San Quentin State Prison in 1959.

The Hillside Stranglers were cousins Kenneth Bianchi and Angelo Buono Jr. They are believed to have killed ten people as a duo and brought terror to Hollywood and Los Angeles in the late 1970s. The pair would pretend to be police detectives and target vulnerable woman. This was a sadistic and sick duo who would rape, torture, and inject their victims with strange drugs. Bianchi and Buono Jr seemed to enjoy experimenting with methods of torture. They used lethal injections and electric shocks on the victims before they strangled them. Their youngest victims were two twelve year-old girls.

Randy Kraft killed dozens of men from 1973 to 1982. He claimed to have killed over sixty people. His targets were hitchhikers - who he would give drugs and alcohol and then often strangle. He was arrested in 1983 after two two traffic cops noticed him driving in an erratic fashion. When they pulled him up he had a dead body in the car with him. Randy Kraft was known as The Scorecard Killer because he kept a tally of his victims in the fashion of a scoresheet. The odd thing about Kraft is that he was intelligent and worked in computers. Those that had known him at school said he was the least likely person to be a serial killer one could imagine.

Richard (The Night Stalker) Ramirez would sometime daub occult symbols in the houses where he had killed. Ramirez left the eyes of one victim in a jewel box for the authorities to find. Ramirez would use anything to hand to kill people. Some victims were killed with a machete or tyre iron. Ramirez nearly decapitated one victim by slashing her in the throat multiple times. John Christie, who gassed, raped, and strangled at 10 Rillington Place, gained the confidence of victims by pretending to have medical knowledge. He would offer to cure ailments like bronchitis and even said he could perform simple abortions.

Colin Ireland was a serial killer active in London in 1993. He killed five gay men by pretending to be gay himself and going home with them. The victims thought they were going to play bondage games with Ireland but once they were restrained he would kill them and rifle through their wallets looking for money. He often forced the victims to reveal their bank card numbers before they died. Ireland had been in trouble with the law from a young age and was always destined to turn out bad. He was said to be a well organised killer who even brought a change of clothes with him for use after each murder. Ireland was apprehended in 1993 and given life in prison. He said he targeted gay men because they were 'easy' victims. He died in prison of natural causes in 2012.

Dennis Nilsen would often creep up behind victims and strangle them with a tie while they were listening to music through headphones. Nilsen said that after one murder he slumped into a chair and listened to O'Superman (a 1981 song by performance artist and musician Laurie Anderson) eight times in a row. Nilsen genuinely seemed to think he was 'honouring' his victims by caring for their dead bodies and performing sexual acts with them. H.H. Holmes is often dubbed America's first serial killer. In the 1890s, he constructed a 'murder castle' above his drug store. This was a windowless room where he could torture and murder. H.H. Holmes picked up some extra money by selling the skeletons of some of his victims to medical schools.

How Do Serial killers Get Rid Of Dead Bodies?

Well, when it comes to disposing of bodies, serial killers vary. Some make an effort to get of evidence and some don't. It really depends on the circumstances of the murder and (in many cases) the intelligence (or indeed mental state) of the killer. A lot of serial killers leave the victims where they killed them and then flee the scene. There are big differences though in the killers who do this. Richard Chase for example would leave blood all over the place after killing someone. He was quite easy to catch because he left hand and footprints all over his crime scenes. Danny Rolling on the other hand, while also a gruesome killer, carried cleaning fluids around with him so that he could clean up his crime scenes and negate the possibility of leaving DNA. Chase was a disorganised serial killer while Rolling (though equally dangerous) was an organised serial killer.

With his early victims, Jeffrey Dahmer used to dissolve the flesh in acid (Dahmer's father was a chemist and so Dahmer always had an interest in science) and then pulverize the bones with a hammer. In 1987, Jeffrey Dahmer woke up in a motel with the dead body of a man next to him. He somehow managed to get the body out of the motel using a suitcase and took it to his grandmother's home (where Dahmer lived) so that he could dissect the body and dispose of it. Later on though, Dahmer ended up trapped in his apartment with an escalating number of bodies that he had no way of disposing of.

People with an interest in true crime are often confused at how killers like Jeffrey Dahmer and Dennis Nilsen lived in apartment buildings and yet no one noticed the smell! The police actually found some incense sticks in Dahmer's apartment. So this WAS how he tried to disguise the smell of his victims. Neigbours of Jeffrey Dahmer did complain about the smell coming from his apartment once. He apparently told them that his fridge broke and some food went bad. Jeffrey Dahmer's apartment was eventually so full with victims and body parts that he put one body in the bath and had to shower over it. The apartment contained a plastic drum of acid where three human torsos were dissolving. The police found a complete skeleton in Jeffrey Dahmer's filing cabinet and three human heads in the fridge.

John Wayne Gacy stuffed the bodies of most of his victims in the crawlspace of his home. When his wife asked about the smell he told her it was mice. Gacy used his experience as a mortician's assistant to block the cavities of his victims with rags and underwear. This prevented too much leakage after death. Gacy told people he had sewer problems if they noticed any foul odour in his house. Gacy is said to have used some sort of chemical dust in his (failed) attempt to disguise the smell coming from his crawlspace. When his crawlspace started to get too full up with bodies, he used his car to throw dead victims off the I-55 bridge into the Des Plaines River.

The crawlspace in Gacy's house was one of the most grim and disturbing sights police detectives were ever likely to witness. Some of the bodies had become fused together in decomposition. Many of John Wayne Gacy's victims were found to have rope tied around their neck. It was an exceptionally complex and time consuming task to identify all of the victims. Sadly, to this day, there are still victims of Gacy yet to be identified.

Serhiy Tkach (aka The Pavlohrad Maniac) was, as you'd expect from someone who worked as a criminal investigator, very shrewd when it came to disposing of victims. He would dump the bodies of victims near highways. This made it look as if the victim had been killed by someone out of town - like a truck driver. The Tool Box Killers Lawrence Sigmund Bittaker and Roy Lewis Norris would throw the bodies of victims into canyons to be eaten by animals. The Hillside Stranglers put one victim in the boot of her car after she was killed and then pushed the vehicle over a cliff. Joel Rifkin used an X-acto knife to cut up his first victim. He cut off the fingertips so that she would be harder to identify if found. Another Rifkin victim was wrapped in plastic, stuffed in a cardboard box and then dumped in the Hudson River. Rifkin also bought some 55 gallon drums in which to store victims. Body parts in a steel drum were later found by a member of the public when they washed ashore.

John George Haigh was a British serial killer known as the Acid Bath Murderer. Haigh was basically a thief and conman who became inspired by the tale of Georges-Alexandre Sarret, a French killer who used sulphuric acid to dispose of victims. Haigh simply deduced (as we noted earlier) that if he killed the people he had robbed and conned and dissolved their bodies in acid then no one would ever be able to finger him for any crimes. Haigh was undone because of his past convictions for theft and fraud. When the police decided to investigate him in relation to some recent crimes they found that Haigh now lived in rooms with no drain access. Haigh had dissolved his latest victim in acid but then covered it in rubble. The police proved there was human fat and remains in the rubble and - as a consequence - Haigh was hung in 1949. The police actually discovered part of a human foot in the rubble.

David Parker Ray (aka The Toy-Box Killer) is estimated to have over fifty women but no bodies were ever found. The reason why they could never find any verifiable victims is that Parker Ray is believed to have disposed of bodies in the Elephant Butte Reservoir (which is a huge man made lake). Juan Corona murdered 25 farm fruit pickers in California in 1971 with a machete and then buried them in the orchards. Other workers noticed the suspicious graves though. Fritz Haarmann (aka The Vampire of Hanover) dumped his victims in the Leine River (a river in Thuringia and Lower Saxony). Some of the bodies washed ashore - which led the police to investigate the river thoroughly. They dragged the river and found hundreds of human bones.

Moses Sithole is known as The ABC Killer because his murders took place in the towns of Atteridgeville, Boksburg, and Cleveland in South Africa. He is credited with 38 murders but (as usual with serial killers) the true number of victims is most likely much higher than that figure. Sithole targeted women of most ages and would isolate them, take them to a quiet rural spot, and then rape and strangle them. He buried the victims in a mass grave near an old mine. In his confession to the police, Fred West complained that Rose West had stuffed the body of one of his daughters in a dustbin. The victims at 25 Cromwell Street were buried in the garden and the basement. Fred West worked as a plasterer and so his building experience came in handy when it came to trying to cover up bodies.

Ahmad Suradji was born in Medan, Indonesia in 1952. Suradji was found to have killed 42 girls and young women on a sugarcane plantation near his home. Suradji considered himself to be a mystical shaman and killed the women as part of a black magic ritual. He buried them up to their heads in the ground, collected their saliva (which he believed gave him magic powers), and then strangled the victims but left them buried with their heads pointing at his house because he believed this ritual gave him extra power. The whole idea for this had apparently come in a message delivered by his late father in a dream. Yes, it's probably safe to say that Ahmad Suradji was absolutely insane.

After he killed for the first time, Dennis Nilsen purchased an electric knife to dismember the victim but couldn't go through with it. He then began to see the beauty (from his point of view) in a dead body and decided to wash and keep the corpses. Nilsen said that when (his first victim) Stephen Holmes was under the floorboards his curiosity got the better of him and he simply had to take a look. This would become a regular feature of Nilsen's murders. The corpse would become like a possession or toy for Nilsen. When he lived at 195 Melrose Avenue, Dennis Nilsen had access to a garden out the back of his flat. He was able to dispose of some of victims by burning them on a bonfire. Nilsen had to throw some tyres onto the bonfire to mask the odour of burning flesh and organs. Dennis Nilsen said he would sometimes vomit in the garden at Melrose Avenue when he was burning the bodies.

When he still lived at 195 Melrose Avenue and had use of a garden, Nilsen would sometimes bury body parts underneath bushes. Dennis Nilsen became skilled at dissecting a human body. This is a grisly but unavoidable task for serial killers who murder at home. Nilsen chopped up some of his victims and stuffed them in the floorboards of his flat at Melrose Avenue. One can only imagine how that place must have smelled. There were a few incidents of neighbours complaining of a smell coming from Nilsen's 195 Melrose Avenue flat. Nilsen told them that the odour stemmed from structural problems in the building. Nilsen was once a victim of burglars and two police detectives came to the flat to investigate. Nilsen was amazed that the detectives didn't notice the foul odour seeped into his home from all the body parts. At one point the detectives were standing directly above the remains of two victims under the floorboards. Nilsen was equally amazed that they didn't notice anything suspicious about him.

Dennis Nilsen said he would sometimes slip some human remains between two fences for them to be eaten by garden animals. When Nilsen was arrested and the story of his murders broke, a Daily Mirror reporter rushed down to Nilsen's old home at Melrose Avenue because he'd heard that the police were going to search the garden there. The reporter spoke to a dog walker who told him that his dog had uncovered some very strange bones in the park that was close to Dennis Nilsen's old garden. Nilsen lived quite near the park in question. He disposed of some remains in this park. Nilsen said he scattered the internal organs of his victims in different places. When he chopped up the bodies of his victims, Dennis Nilsen had to strip to his underwear to avoid getting stains on his clothes.

Nilsen sometimes put the torsos of victims in suitcases until he had a chance to burn them. Near Melrose Avenue, a man is alleged to have once found a ripped plastic bag that seemed to contain a rib-cage. The man did not report this (presumably because it hadn't occurred to him that the bones might be human). The bonfires that Nilsen had at Melrose Avenue would burn for hours long into the night. When he had bonfires to burn remains, Nilsen used lighter fuel to make sure he got a good blaze going. After one of his bonfires at Melrose Avenue, Nilsen said he had to crush a skull with a rake.

Because he didn't drive, disposing of remains and bodies was a constant struggle for Dennis Nilsen. Ted Bundy and Gary Ridgeway would leave the bodies of their victims in the woods or a forest and go back and have sex with them until such time as decomposition made this impossible. We see similar behaviour in Dennis Nilsen - although his victims were always in his flats. Dennis Nilsen's last home was at Flat 23D Cranley Gardens, Muswell Hill. Nilsen's attic flat at Cranley Gardens was very cramped. All the ceilings were sloped. The crime scene photographs of this flat after Nilsen's arrest show it be a claustrophobic and squalid place. When he moved to Cranley Gardens, Nilsen no longer had access to garden and so disposing of the bodies became much more difficult.

You had to go up three flights of stairs to get Nilsen's flat at Cranley Gardens. Although he said he couldn't stand the sight of blood, Nilsen clearly had a strong stomach. He was capable of cutting bodies in half, hacking off limbs, and boiling heads. When he had a dead body under the floorboards, Nilsen would spray insecticide and deodorant down there twice a day. It is speculated that Nilsen wasn't too bothered the awful smell of his flat at Cranley Gardens in the end because he had become used to it. The windows were always open - even in the winter. Nilsen, inspired by John Haigh, said that he considered dissolving the remains of his victims in the bath but never went ahead with this because it was impracticable. He had no idea where to get hold of vast quantities of acid and knew it would be a highly suspicious thing to try and purchase or use.

Nilsen once dropped a carrier bag of human remains in the street by accident when he was walking his dog. The remains were found by a member of the public and reported but nothing came of this. After he boiled the head of a victim, Nilsen would pick off the flesh and put it down the toilet. The process of boiling flesh was very time consuming. Nilsen must have spent hours doing this. Dennis Nilsen ended up in an identical situation to Jeffrey Dahmer. They both ended up trapped in a top floor apartment festooned with body parts that they couldn't dispose of. Nilsen said he would cut through torsos at the waist. He quickly learned what the quickest way to cut up a body was.

Dennis Nilsen would boil hands and feet for hours to separate the flesh from the bones. He would put the bones in the dustbin. Nilsen would sometimes flush pieces of flesh that weighed two pounds down the toilet. It genuinely didn't seem to occur to Nilsen that he might be storing up trouble by putting flesh down the toilet. Nilsen was captured because a plumbing company was called out to unblock the drain outside his building at Cranley Gardens. When he first heard that someone was having trouble flushing the toilet at Cranley Gardens, Nilsen didn't realise at first that he had caused the blockage by flushing remains down the toilet. He was rather slow on the uptake. Tests on the bones and remains blocking the drain found that they were human and the drainpipe led directly to Nilsen's flat.

Mike Cattran was the Dyno-Rod employee called out to unblock the drain outside Nilsen's apartment building. He said the smell of human decay when he lifted up the manhole cover was overwhelming. Nilsen tried to suggest to Mike Cattran that the drains to his building must be blocked with fast food. This ruse obviously didn't work. After Dyno-Rod were called out to unblock the drain, Nilsen made an attempt to remove bones and flesh from the drain himself but it was too late. The flesh and bones that clogged the drains and led to Nilsen's capture had attracted a lot of rats. When the police searched Nilsen's flat they encountered a nightmarish scene. Nielsen had body parts and torsos hidden all over the place. He even had bags containing the heads of some of his victims. The police found mothballs in one of the bags containing remains of Nilsen's victims. Mothballs are small balls of chemical pesticide and deodorant used when storing clothing and other articles susceptible to damage from mold.

Rodney (The Dating Game Killer) Alcala was very adept at leaving no forensic evidence. He would lure girls for a photography session and then murder them. The police found hundreds of photographs of these girls but finding the bodies and remains was another matter entirely. Many of his possible victims remain unidentified. Ted Bundy was also quite a shrewd sort of killer. Bundy's fingerprints were never found at a crime scene. H.H. Holmes was one of the smartest killers when it came to getting rid of victims. Holmes had an incinerator in the basement for disposing of bodies. The Suffolk Strangler dumped two of his victims in a stream or river. This was quite shrewd (if intentional) because water will obviously wash away DNA evidence.

Dean Corll was a former U.S army repairman who killed 28 young men between 1970 and 1973. Many of Dean Corll's victims were disposed of via his boat shed on the Sam Rayburn Reservoir. William Bonin, who confessed to 21 murders and was executed in 1996, would often dump his victims in some trash after he had killed them. Oba Chandler was a killer executed for three murders he committed in Florida in 1989. This was an especially heartless crime. Chandler had met a female tourist who was on vacation in Florida with her two teenage daughters. Chandler took them out on a cruise and then threw them into the sea one by one tied up in ropes with cement weights. Chandler is widely believed to have been responsible for other unsolved murders.

Steven Grieveson is a serial killer known as the Sunderland Strangler. He killed three teenage boys in the early 1990s. Steven Grieveson was not much older than his victims. He strangled one with his own bandana and tried to burn the victims. The deaths were not deemed suspicious at first but a local detective thankfully managed to establish a link. Grieveson was gay but did not want anyone to know he was gay. This was the most likely motivation for the murders because there was evidence of sexual contact with the victims.

A lot of serial killers seem to think that burning bodies is a good idea but this method is less successful than you might think. They always tend to get caught.

Generally, there are all sorts of methods killers use to get rid of bodies. The most effective is simply to dump them in a large river or the sea. Many killers in America leave the victims in a forest where a lot of decomposition will occur before they are found. Other killers (especially city dwellers) will just leave the bodies where they are - often because they love the thought of leaving a shocking crime scene. And then you get the killers like Dahmer and Nilsen who end up in a the nightmarish and surreal situation of living in a flat where the cupboards and drawers are full up with body parts and human flesh. As with everything else, serial killers don't really conform to any one method or strategy when it comes to getting rid of bodies.

Which Serial Killers Inspired Movies?

This topic is literally a book unto itself. There have been endless biopics about serial killers in film and on television and countless films that take inspiration from real life killers. The horror genre is naturally something that lends itself to inspiration from grisly real life killers. These serial killer inspired productions run the full spectrum from prime time prestige TV to grubby exploitation or straight to DVD clunkers. Some of the serial killer inspired TV shows and movies are very good and some are completely terrible. An example of a high end top quality serial killer inspired production would be the David Fincher produced Netflix show Mindhunter. This show revolves around the FBI's Behavioral Science Unit. The characters have to interview real incarcerated serial killers and so you get depictions of notorious killers like Ed Kemper, Richard Speck, Dennis Rader, and Jerry Brudos in the series. Mindhunter is worth watching for anyone with an interest in true crime.

The Wolf Creek horror films were loosely based on Ivan Milat - a serial killer who murdered backpackers in the Australian outback. Milat was every bit as brutal and terrifying as Mick Taylor in the Wolf Creek films. Gary Heidnik was executed in 1999 for the murder, torture, and rape of six women in 1986 and 1987. He would keep the captives prisoner in a pit at the base of his house. Buffalo Bill in The Silence of the Lambs was partly based on Heidnik. Hannibal Lector is the most famous fictional serial killer. He is based on several killers but was also largely inspired by a sinister doctor that Thomas Harris once met.

The skin masks and suits that Ed Gein fashioned from his graverobbing activities were obviously the inspiration for Leatherface in the Texas Chainsaw Massacre films. Gein's unfathomable crimes spawned a number of films (sometimes loosely) based on his exploits - Psycho, The Silence of the Lambs, Deranged, In the Light of the Moon (which stars Steve Railsback as Gein). 1974's Deranged stars Roberts Blossom as Ezra Cobb (Cobb is clearly based on Gein), a nutty rural chap who exhumes his mother and begins abducting and killing local women. Deranged is a bit rough around the edges (it plainly didn't have much of a budget) but it's quite an effective little horror film. 2000's In the Light of the Moon is also worth watching. Although hardly a classic, In the Light of the Moon serves as a fairly accurate depiction of Ed Gein's crimes and is always fairly compelling. Ed Gein's unusual home decor and bone and skin themed bric-a-brac was also clearly a big influence on the classic 1974 film The Texas Chainsaw Massacre. Yes, it's safe to say that Ed Gein has been a big inspiration when it comes to horror films.

A fairly well received television movie about John Wayne Gacy called To Catch a Killer was made in 1992. It starred the always reliable Brian Dennehy as Gacy. Gacy was killed by lethal injection a few years after the film. In 2003 there was another film about this killer simply entitled Gacy. Mark Holton played Gacy in this straight to DVD film. It got terrible reviews. A third Gacy film is 2010's Dear Mr Gacy. This film is based on a memoir by Jason Moss. Moss corresponded with Gacy when Gacy was in prison in an attempt to learn more about serial killers. He even personally met Gacy in prison (and found Gacy to be a powerful and manipulative sociopath). William Forsythe played Gacy in this watchable drama. Believe it or not there is even a horror film called Dahmer vs. Gacy where these two killers are cloned, get loose, and do battle. Though played for laughs, Dahmer vs. Gacy is strictly bottom of the barrel amateur hour and best avoided.

The first actor to play Ted Bundy was Mark Harmon in the 1986 NBC television film The Deliberate Stranger. The actor Robert Hays (who you might know from the Airplane! comedy spoof films) was originally asked to play Ted Bundy in The Deliberate Stranger but felt it was a distasteful project and wanted no part of it. The Deliberate Stranger is very good on the whole - though of course diluted for television (you won't get to see too much of Bundy killing anyone). What the film does well is show us how Bundy (with his plaster of Paris ruse where he would pretend to have a broken arm and ask women to help carry his library books to his car) could be quite charming. He managed to lull victims into a false sense of security.

'Although The Deliberate Stranger might appear slow to some,' wrote Diaboliquemagazine, 'it has more in common with this modern aesthetic than its competition at the time and this helps it still feel fresh. Added to this is the sense of time and place, and because it is set in the time the events happened, it avoids being dated. We're also more used these days to long-form storytelling with season-long shows about single crimes. Or, in cinema, the slow, measured approach of something like David Fincher's Zodiac. Now, The Deliberate Stranger is not a small-screen Fincher but it does show the influence of a number of '70s crime films that gave it more ambition than much contemporary TV. It uses the tools of true crime journalism and the core of the police procedural to slowly reveal Bundy to us. It's a strong piece of work that never attempts to humanize Bundy but uses its scope, attention to detail and relative freedom in running time to compel us and in that, it succeeds.'

Michael Reilly Burke was the second actor to portray Ted Bundy. He played Bundy in the 2002 Matthew Bright film Ted Bundy. This second Bundy film is not bad but never quite distinguishes itself or ever really justifies its existence. The film plays rather loose with the Bundy story and Burke also seems a little over the top at times. You could believe that Mark Harmon's Bundy could hide in plain sight all the time but you don't get that sense with the depiction of Bundy by Michael Reilly Burke. The film is rather silly at times - especially in the sequence where Bundy goes to the electric chair.

Despite my own lukewarm reception to the 2002 Ted Bundy

film it did receive some positive critical notices and is probably worth a look if you are curious. 'Matthew Bright is extraordinarily accurate in the minutiae of detail,' wrote Moria, 'from depicting Bundy's favourite gimmick of using the cast on his arm to ask women for help, to the story where he tried to impersonate a police officer to abduct Carol DaRonch, even the infamous yellow VW Bug. (The girlfriend played by Boti Ann Bliss actually existed – she even later wrote a book about her relationship with Bundy, The Phantom Prince: My Life with Ted Bundy (1981), under the pseudonym Elizabeth Kendall). Every murder that is seen throughout the film restages killings that Ted Bundy conducted, which Matthew Bright replicates even down to mentioning minor details such as Bundy biting his victims and beating them with a log during the attack on the Chi Omega sorority house in Tallahassee.'

Billy Campbell was the third person to play Ted Bundy. This was in the competent but routine 2003 TV film adaptation of Ann Rule's book The Stranger Beside Me. Ann Rule worked with Bundy on a suicide hotline and considered him to be a friend. The Bundy she knew was kind and considerate. You can imagine then her shock when she found out that Bundy was a serial killer - and one of the worst ones in American history to boot. Campbell is effective enough as Bundy although like Mark Harmon he's probably a trifle too Hollywood handsome for the part. Campbell's performance works because he underplays Bundy and doesn't ever resort to chewing up the scenery.

The Riverman is a 2004 television film based on Robert Keppel's 2004 non-fiction book The Riverman: Ted Bundy and I Hunt For the Green River Killer. It was written by Tom Towler and directed by Bill Eagles. Bruce Greenwood plays Keppel and Cary Elwes plays Ted Bundy. Gary Ridgway (the 'Green River' serial killer that Keppel is hunting) doesn't really feature much in the film and is played by Dave Brown. The story is more about how Keppel became intrigued by Bundy and how being in close proximity to such an evil man affected him. The focus of the film is on Keppel and The Riverman is absorbing enough as TV movies go. Bundy doesn't feature much - which is sort of refreshing because we don't have to trawl through the (already too familiar by now) Ted Bundy story yet again. We merely meet Bundy in prison a few times in this TV movie.

'Although The Riverman is about the hunt for Ridgway,' wrote Scriptophobic, 'and partly about Bundy, its true focus remains on Keppel throughout and his state of mind becomes the device priming the film's engine. Many films based on real serial killers focus on the grim details of the murders involved, or the personalities and lives of the killers. This one chooses to examine what effects those details have on people whose job it is to be immersed in them. Not to say we're wrong for taking interest in stories involving serial murder— this column wouldn't exist otherwise. Films like The Riverman, few though they may be, remind us that vicious predators like Bundy and Ridgway are not meant to be glorified. It's the people who honour their victims by hunting and chasing their killers who ought to be examined, remembered, and honoured.'

The Capture of the Green River Killer was a 2008 TV movie (again) about the Gary Ridgway case. James Marsters played Ted Bundy and John Pielmeier played Gary Ridgway. The Capture of the Green River Killer has some decent reviews although I'm not quite sure why we needed two television movies about the same subject. The Riverman was perfectly competent and would have sufficed on its own. Corin Nemec then became the latest actor to play Ted Bundy in the 2008 film Bundy: An American Icon. This was by far the weakest of the Bundy films because it was less a drama and more of a schlocky straight to DVD horror film. Bundy: An American Icon was pretty awful by any standards. Nemec looks far too old to be playing Ted Bundy (this is obviously even more pronounced in the college scenes) and the film features hammy acting and headache inducing flashbacks. Horror icon Kane Hodder even turns up as a judge at the trial - which probably tells you all you need to know about how serious a film Bundy: An American Icon turns out to be.

Zac Effron became the last (at the time of writing) actor to play Ted Bundy in the 2019 Netflix film Extremely Wicked, Shockingly Evil, and Vile. The film is based on Elizabeth Kloepfer's book The Phantom Prince and takes its title from the closing comments of the Judge in Bundy's trial - "The court finds that both of these killings were indeed heinous, atrocious and cruel. And that they were extremely wicked, shockingly evil, vile and the product of a design to inflict a high degree of pain and utter indifference to human life." Lily Collins portrays Bundy's girlfriend Liz Kendall (Elizabeth Kloepfer) in the movie. The film is about Elizabeth Kloepfer's growing suspicion of Bundy although the story seems to lose focus and drift from this at some point. You don't get to see Bundy kill anyone in the movie but there is a very gripping sequence depicting Bundy's escape from the courthouse library.

Extremely Wicked, Shockingly Evil, and Vile has the best production values of any Ted Bundy film and a terrific cast but the general consensus is that the film (though well made) didn't really justify its existence or tell us anything we didn't already know about this already well chronicled maniac. I would imagine that most true crime buffs have read The Phantom Prince and are familiar with the story of Ted Bundy and so you can't help feeling that Extremely Wicked, Shockingly Evil, and Vile won't tell anyone anything they didn't already know. The trial scenes near the end are very good though - in no small way thanks to John Malkovich as Judge Edward Cowart. The verbal jousting between Bundy and Cowart is very compelling in the movie.

The character of Patrick Bateman in the Bret Easton Ellis book (and later film) American Pyscho clearly owes a lot to Ted Bundy. Robert Keppel, who wrote the book The Riverman: Ted Bundy and I Hunt For the Green River Killer, was the inspiration for Will Graham. Dennis Radar was the inspiration for the Stephen King story A Good Marriage in his Full Dark, No Stars collection. This story was later turned into a solid enough movie. Greg Henry played Dennis Rader in The Hunt for the BTK Killer - a dire 2006 TV movie. Horror icon Kane Hodder also played Rader (or a character named Dennis at least) in the equally awful 2009 film B.T.K.

John Backderf, who knew Jeffrey Dahmer at school, wrote a comic called My Friend Dahmer - which was later turned into a film. My Friend Dahmer is certainly a well made and interesting film that is worth watching. Backderf said there was always a darkness about Dahmer and he wasn't the sort of person you'd want to be alone with. Believe it or not, Marvel star Jeremy Renner played Jeffrey Dahmer is a 2002 film simply called Dahmer. Dhamer got decent reviews. There are at least two other Dahmer films but none of them are worth watching.

Graham Young was known as The Teacup Poisoner. He was sent to Broadmoor in 1962 for poisoning his family and killing his stepmother. Deemed cured, he was released nine years later and secured work at a laboratory. Soon, the work colleagues of Young began to fall mysteriously ill. He had of course been poisoning them as part of his chemical experiments! Young was arrested in 1971 and found to have dangerous chemicals on him. He was sentenced to life in prison and died in 1990. Young killed at least three people (the true tally is probably higher) and made many more terribly ill. He was found to have kept a detailed diary of his experiments. A brilliant 1995 film called The Young Poisoner's Handbook was based on Graham Young. The version of Young depicted in the film though is more likeable than the real person. The real Graham Young was said to be obsessed with Nazis and became friends with the Moors Murderer Ian Brady at Broadmoor.

The first Jack the Ripper film is believed to be The Lodger in 1926. This was Alfred Hitchcock's adaptation of the Marie Belloc Lowndes novel. There have been more films about Jack the Ripper than any other real life killer. The eclectic band of films and TV shows inspired by the Ripper includes A Study in

Terror (an enjoyable 1965 film where Sherlock Holmes attempts to find the Ripper), Hammer's Hands of the Ripper, Murder by Decree (another film which blends fiction and fact by having Sherlock Holmes inhabit the same universe as the Ripper), and endless others - including an Italian-Spanish giallo film based on the notorious murderer. TV hows like Whitechapel and Ripper Street have been inspired by the case. Michael Caine starred in a decent (if TV sanitised) 1988 Jack the Ripper miniseries and the Ripper has even been transplanted to modern day America in silly films like Jack's Back. If you are interested in Jack the Ripper you must read Alan Moore's brilliant graphic novel From Hell if you haven't done so already. From Hell later inspired a terrible film adaptation with Johnny Depp.

Richard Kuklinski from Jersey City claimed to have murdered someone for the first time when he was thirteen. He claimed to be a mob hitman who killed 300 people. Kuklinski was motivated not by lust but the enjoyment of killing. He was first apprehended on other charges in the 1980s. Though a film (The Iceman) has been made based on his life, some crime writers are dubious that Kuklinski's claims of being a mass killer are verifiable. The 1986 film Henry: Portrait of a Serial Killer was based on Ottiss Toole and Henry Lee Lucas. Ottis Toole was a Florida born serial killer who confessed to over a hundred murders (he was officially convicted of six murders at his trial but DNA evidence suggested this was merely the tip of the iceberg). He is believed to have gone on a killing spree with Henry Lee Lucas. Toole had a very low IQ and his mother was said to be crazy and involved in occult rituals. Though sentenced to death, the execution was never carried out and Toole died in prison in 1996 at the age of 49.

The Boston Strangler case involved 13 women (of varying ages) being murdered in Boston between 1962 and 1964. The killer used a nylon stocking to strangle many of his victims. Albert DeSalvo was convicted for the Boston Strangler murders. DeSalvo may have raped as many as 300 women and confessed to the Strangler killings. There are those though who feel the murders were too eclectic in nature to have all been carried out by one man. Tony Curtis played Albert DeSalvo in a film based on the Boston Strangler case. The movie version of this notorious case is well regarded and worth watching. Charlize Theron won an Oscar for portraying Aileen Wuornos in the 2003 film Monster. The never captured Zodiac Killer inspired David Fincher's gripping 2007 film Zodiac. Monster and Zodiac are both very good. Zodiac in particular is one of the best true crime movies in recent memory.

The Bloody Benders were a family of serial killers who lived in Labette County, Kansas. From 1871 to 1872 they are believed to have murdered around 20 people. The weird thing about the Bloody Benders is that the mother and daughter were a full part of the murders. Kate Bender, the daughter, would lure men to their house (which was a sort of general store) and Ma Bender would cook for them. While they were eating, the victims would be hit by a sledgehammer and have their throat cut. The motive for the murders was robbery. The Bloody Benders had their ruse uncovered when they killed a doctor. The brothers of the doctor organised a huge search for him in the area and the Bender home was searched. It was found to contain bodies which had been sent through a trapdoor. The locals burned down the Bender home. And the Bender family? They had vanished. No one really knows what happened to them. The Bloody Benders feel like an obvious inspiration for the nutty Sawyer family in the Texas Chainsaw Massacre films.

David Berkowitz inspired Spike Lee's somewhat forgettable film Son of Sam. A Berkowitz inspired film is that is worth watching is the TV movie Out of the Darkness with Martin Sheen. John Cusack played Alaska wilderness serial killer Robert Hansen in the so-so 2013 film The Frozen Ground. The film Citzen X with Donald Sutherland is worth watching. This film is about the efforts to catch Andrei Chikatilo. Chikatilo is played by Jeffrey DeMunn. The 2009 film Slaughter was inspired by Belle Gunness. The South Korean serial killer Yoo Young-chul inspired the 2008 film The Chaser. The 1990 French film Doctor Petiot is based on the case of Marcel Petiot.

Marcel Petiot was the doctor of a town in France during World War 2. He offered sanctuary to Jews fleeing the authorities and then killed them with a shot of poison. He confessed to 60 murders when the war ended and he was arrested.

2007 saw a terrible film called Chicago Massacre: Richard Speck come out. Speck was played by Corin Nemec - who had already played Ted Bundy in another forgettable serial killer biopic. Richard Speck was infamous for the torture and murder of eight student nurses from South Chicago Community Hospital in July 1966. Speck went into a student nursing dormitory and tied the women up. He raped, tortured, and killed them. One nurse survived by hiding under a bed. Speck was already known to the police for thirty previous arrests. He was known as a thief who robbed people at knifepoint. Speck claimed to be intoxicated on drugs when he murdered the nurses. The 1983 Charles Bronson action thriller film 10 to Midnight also seems to have been inspired by Richard Speck (and Ted Bundy too).

A film was actually made about Dennis Nilsen in 1989 called Cold Light of Day. However, the film is so amateurish it was quicky forgotten. Cold Light of Day was directed by Fhiona-Louise and features Bob Flag as Nilsen (called Jordan March in the film though clearly based on Nilsen). The film is a rather grim experience. It shows Nilsen/March strangling people and boiling heads. The Allslightsceserved blog wrote of Cold Light of Day - 'Cold Light of Day, despite the involvement as producer of horror stalwart Richard Driscoll - writer/director of such reviled work as The Comic (1985) and Kannibal (2001) - is not a piece of exploitative kitsch. Admittedly it does deviate from the facts of the Nilsen case; only three murders are committed here and the otherwise effective Bob Flag is slightly too old for the role, given Nilsen was only 37 at the time of his arrest. But its portrayal of a lonely, desolate world of dingy pubs and greasy spoons, where people in need of comfort are driven to extraordinary lengths, is a deeply an unsettling one. We watch Jordan interacting with his fellow tenants and even taking steps to ensure an elderly neighbour receives proper care and support. He's the kind of ordinary, seemingly decent bloke who might live down your street, and that true horror sometimes lurks behind the most banal exteriors.'

There was a fresh wave of interest in Dennis Nilsen in 2020 when the acclaimed ITV drama Des was broadcast. Former Doctor Who actor David Tennant played Nilsen. ITV received a smattering of complaints about their drama Des but not too many. The drama was fairly restrained and respectful. It didn't feature Nilsen strangling people and chopping up bodies or anything like that. David Tennant said he was relieved that Dennis Nilsen died before the drama Des was broadcast because he believed Nilsen would probably have derived some pleasure at being the centre of attention again. The greatest punishment for Nilsen after his arrest was that he was sort of forgotten. He wasn't allowed to be interviewed and later British killers like Ian Huntley, Harold Shipman and Fred West became more famous than him. Des is a very compelling television drama and well worth watching.

The Clint Eastwood film Dirty Harry was inspired by the Zodiac killings. Plans to make feature films about the Moors Murders (believe it or not the American film director William Friedkin was once attached to a Moors Murders film) and the Yorkshire Ripper were shelved in the end because they were deemed too controversial. Alferd Packer has inspired a number of films including Trey Parker and Matt Stone's Cannibal! The Musical and the cult 1998 horror movie Ravenous. The classic Alfred Hitchcock film Frenzy was heavily inspired by the Jack the Stripper murders. It is sometimes suggested that Michael Myers in the Halloween films is based on Edwward Kemper. This is not true. John Carpenter based Michael Myers on a 'devil eyed' child he saw in a mental institution. Francis Dolarhyde in the novel Red Dragon was based on Dennis Rader. Wes Craven's Scream was inspired by the student slasher Danny Rolling.

Lou Diamond Phillips played Richard Ramirez in the 2016

film The Night Stalker. This film got fairly lukewarm reviews. Ramirez was also played by George Kiseleff in a straight to DVD abomination by Ulli Lommel in 2005. Lommel also made straight to DVD turkeys about the Zodiac Killer and Robert Pickton (the Canadian serial killer who chopped his victims up and fed his pigs with them). The Richard Ramirez story also inspired the terrible 2002 horror cheapie Nightstalker. The story of Leonard Lake and Charles Ng also got the terrible cheapie straight to DVD treatment in the 2012 film House on the Hill. William Bonin, Ed Kemper, and Danny Rolling are other killers who have been subject to low-budget straight to DVD films.

Somewhat better than straight to DVD nonsense was the 2017 film Dating Game Killer - where Guillermo Díaz played Rodney Alcala. The Hillside Strangers got the film treatment in the tepid 2004 film The Hillside Strangler. The film starred C. Thomas Howell as Bianchi and Nicholas Turturro as Buono. A much better film based on this case was the 1989 TV film The Case of the Hillside Stranglers. The mediocre 2009 horror film Berdella starred Seth Correa as the infamous Bob Berdella. Richard Attenborough played John Christie in the grim but compelling 1971 film 10 Rillington Place. 10 Rillington Place was remade for television in 2016 with Tim Roth as Christie. Patrick Bauchau played Albert Fish in the largely forgotten 2007 drama The Gray Man. The well received 1995 German film Deathmaker (Der Totmacher) tells the story of the notorious serial killer Fritz Haarmann.

James Bolam played Harold Shipman in a well received British television drama. Dr Harold Shipman was a GP in Manchester who murdered (at least) 218 of his patients with injections of diamorphine (heroin) from 1975 to 1998. He was known as Doctor Death in the British media when his shocking secret came to light. The 2011 TV movie Hunt for the I-5 Killer is a watchable enough drama about the operation to capture Randall Woodfield. The 2007 British television drama See No Evil: The Moors Murders (and based of course on the awful case of killers Ian Brady and Myra Hindley) won a BAFTA for best drama.

There have been a number of films based on the case of Charles Manson and the Manson Family. Helter Skelter with Steve Railsback and Once Upon A Time in Hollywood are both very worthy of your time. The story of John George Haigh was told in the 2002 British television film A Is for Acid. Martin Clunes played Haigh in the film. The 1996 film Killer: A Journal of Murder with James Woods was based on the serial killer Carl Panzram. The Gemini Killer in (the very underrated) The Exorcist III is inspired by the Zodiac killer. The 1987 William Friedkin film Rampage stars Michael Biehn as a killer whose delusions cause him to drink the blood of his victims. This film is obviously (loosely) based on Richard Chase.

We've barely scratched the surface when it comes to serial killer inspired films. There are millions of them and new ones constantly coming out all the time. There have been some great serial killer films but you do have to sift through a lot of dreck to get to them. The general rule is to avoid the straight to DVD horror cheapies as they tend to be awful. The television films and television dramas based on serial killers are usually vastly superior and many of these are well worth watching.

What Were The Last Meals of Serial Killers Before They Were Executed?

Is is of course a longstanding custom that a condemned prisoner about to be executed is granted a last meal. They can, within reason, choose one last special meal to eat before they are put to death. There are variations but this custom still prevails today. Most of the famous last meal requests in true crime reside in the United States because other western nations have long since abolished the death penalty. It is not quite true that condemned prisoners can order whatever they want as a last meal. Sometimes they are limited to what the prison chefs can actually find or cook themselves. In Florida, the last meal is not allowed to exceed $40 and must be procured locally. In some states the budget for the last meal is even lower.

Generally though, the request of a condemned prisoner will usually be catered to as long as it isn't too elaborate or rare - although in some cases some very elaborate last meal requests have been granted as we shall see in this chapter. It is unavoidably fascinating of course to see what famous killers chose as their last ever meal on planet Earth. In 2012, the journal Appetite published a study of last meals by condemned prisoners in the United States from 2002 to 2006. The average last meal came in at 2,756 calories but there were cases of a last meal clocking in at 7,000 calories. 70% of last meal requests ordered fried food. The most popular beverage (alcohol is not usually permitted) was Coca-Cola. 17% of last meal requests asked for Coca-Cola to drink. The most popular last meal request overall in the United States is cheeseburger and fries. The most popular dessert request is ice cream.

Prisons in Texas abandoned the tradition of the last meal for condemned prisoners in 2011. There are a couple of reasons why they did this. The first was the fact that there were documented cases of prisoners receiving a last meal but then being reprieved at the last minute. Prisons clearly got a bit tired of laying on last meals for prisoners who (thanks to appeals) were then not even executed anyway. Another reason why lawmakers and prison officials in Texas dropped the last meal request was the convicted murderer Lawrence Russell Brewer. For his last meal in a Texas prison, the condemned Brewer requested chicken-fried steaks, one pound of barbecued meat, a triple-patty bacon cheeseburger, a meat-lover's pizza, three fajitas, an omelet, a bowl of okra, one pint of Blue Bell Ice Cream, some peanut-butter fudge with crushed peanuts and three root beers. However, when this feast finally arrived Brewer never actually ate a single bite of it.

John Wayne Gacy, who murdered 33 teenage boys and young men between 1972 and 1978, was once the manager of three KFC (or Kentucky fried Chicken as it was known at the time) restaurants. It seems appropriate then that for his last meal on death row, John Wayne Gacy requested 12 fried shrimp, a bucket of original recipe KFC, French fries, and strawberries. Gacy was even allowed to have a picnic with his family before his execution. William Bonin was known as The Freeway Killer for the way he would pick up hitchhikers and then murder them. He murdered over 20 people in the late seventies and early eighties. He was killed by lethal injection in 1996. For his last meal on death row, William Bonin requested pepperoni and sausage pizza, chocolate ice cream, and both Coca-Cola and Pepsi.

John Martin Scripps was an Englishman who murdered three tourists in Singapore and Thailand. British tabloids called him The Tourist From Hell. Scripps used butchery knives to dismember his victims. He was executed in Singapore in 1996. This made him only the second Westerner to be given the death sentence in Singapore since the country became independent. John Martin Scripps chose pizza and hot chocolate for his last meal before he was executed. Joseph "Mad Dog" Taborsky was a killer who left several people dead after a spate of violent robberies. He was killed by electric chair in 1960. For his last meal he had a banana split (an American ice cream-based dessert), cherry soda, and some coffee with cream and sugar. Taborsky obviously had a sweet tooth if his last meal request is anything to go by.

Danny Harold Rolling was born in 1954 in Shreveport, Louisiana. Rolling, who became known as The Gainsville Ripper, was (as we noted in the movie section) one of the inspirations for the Wes Craven movie Scream. Rolling had a habit of stalking and killing students. He was executed by lethal injection at Florida State Prison on October 25, 2006. Rolling requested Lobster tail, butterfly shrimp, baked potato, strawberry cheesecake, and sweet tea for his last meal. Oscar Ray Bolin was convicted of murdering three women in the 1980s but then had the guilty verdict overturned. However, it was then reversed and he was convicted again. He died by lethal injection in 2016. Oscar Ray Bolin's last meal was a rib eye steak, a baked potato with sour cream, a salad, garlic bread, Coca-Cola, and a lemon meringue pie.

Marion Albert Pruett was an American serial killer who killed at least five people. He was killed by lethal injection in Cummins Unit, Arkansas in 1999. For his last meal on death row, Marion Albert Pruett requested four Whoppers from Burger King, a stuffed crust pizza from Pizza Hut, fries, fried eggplant, fried squash, fried okra, a pecan pie, and Pepsi. Pruett had originally asked for roast duck but the prison he was in declined to cook this. John Joubert was an American serial killer convicted of murdering three boys in Maine and Nebraska. He was killed by the electric chair in 1996. For his last meal he chose pizza with green pepper and onions, strawberry cheesecake, and Coca-Cola. Velma Barfield was executed in 1984 by lethal injection for killing her two husbands (and more besides). Barfield had one of the more basic last meal requests. For her last meal she simply asked for some Coca-Cola and a bag of Cheez Doodles.

Kenneth McDuff was an American serial killer convicted in 1966. He is believed to have been responsible for over ten murders. McDuff was executed in 1998 by lethal injection. For his last meal he had two t-bone steaks. Peter Kürten was born in Cologne, Germany, in 1883. He is usually known as The Vampire of Dusseldorf. Peter Kürten was found guilty of murder and attempted murder and executed by guillotine on 2 July 1931. For his last meal before execution he chose Wiener schnitzel, fried potatoes and a bottle of white wine. Gary Ray Bowles killed six men in 1994 along the Interstate 95 highway. He was executed in 2019 at Florida State Prison. For his last meal he had three cheeseburgers with French fries and bacon. Ronnie Lee Gardner was executed in 2010 for two counts of murder. For his last meal he had lobster tail, steak, apple pie and vanilla ice cream.

Gary Heidnik was executed in 1999 for the murder, torture, and rape of six women in 1986 and 1987. For his last meal, Heidnik had two slices of cheese pizza and two cups of black coffee. Raymond Fernandez murdered an estimated 10+ victims with his lover and accomplice and Martha Beck in the late 1940s. Fernandez died in the electric chair in 1951. For his last meal Fernandez had an onion omelet, French fries, some chocolate candy, and a Cuban cigar. Paul Ezra Rhoades was executed by lethal injection in Idaho in 2011 after being convicted of six murders. For his last meal, Rhoades had hot dogs with sauerkraut, mustard, ketchup, onions, relish, baked beans, veggie sticks, and ranch dressing. For his dessert, Rhoades had fruit with gelatin and strawberry ice cream cups.

Gerald Stano claimed to have killed over forty women. He was killed by electric chair in 1998 in Florida State Prison. For his last meal, Gerald Stano had steak, baked potato, salad with blue cheese dressing, lima beans, mint chocolate-chip ice cream, and Pepsi. Bobby Joe Long was a serial killer whose murder spree took place in the Tampa area. Long confessed to eight murders but was eventually convicted of more than that. He was executed in 2019 by lethal injection. For his last meal, Long requested beef, bacon, French fries, and soda. California murderer Clarence Ray Allen requested for his last meal a buffalo steak, KFC, and pecan pie with black-walnut ice cream.

As per his instructions, the pie and ice cream were sugar free.

Fritz Haarmann was born in Hanover, Germany in 1879. In true crime circles he is known as The Vampire of Hanover. The trial of Fritz Haarmann took place in 1924. It didn't last very long. He was found guilty of 24 murders and sentenced to death by beheading. For his last meal, Haarmann simply requested a cup of coffee and a Cuban cigar. A man named James Edward Smith once requested a lump of dirt as his last meal on death row because he wanted to perform a black magic ritual with the soil. His request was declined. In case you were wondering, he ended up having some yogurt as his last meal - which was a rather odd selection. Who would choose yogurt as their last meal? Steven Howard Oken was an American killer who was executed in Maryland by lethal injection in 2004. His last meal was a chicken patty, potatoes, gravy, green beans, marble cake, milk, and fruit punch. This was the regular prison lunch that day so Oken didn't really get a special last meal.

Westley Allan Dodd was an American serial killer who moved to Vancouver. His early years were full of incidents where he molested boys. When he moved to Vancouver, Dodd found that David Douglas Park was ideal for his depraved urges. In 1989 he moved from molestation to murder when he killed two brothers (ages ten and eleven) in the park. He tied them to a tree and stabbed them after he had molested them. Dodd then went to Portland and abducted and killed a four year-old boy. Dodd was captured when he tried to abduct a six year-old boy from a cinema in Washington. The staff intervened and Dodd ran away. The (very brave) boyfriend of the boy's mother chased Dodd's car down and managed to restrain him. When the police searched the home of Dodd, they found a rack for torture, diaries with details of his crimes, and photographs of children. He was charged with three murders and one attempted kidnapping. Dodd was executed in 1993. For his last meal he had salmon and potatoes. Dodd's last meal must rank as one of the healthiest any condemned prisoner has ever chosen! They usually go for burgers and ice cream.

Sean Sellers was an American killer who was convicted of three murders when he was not yet eighteen. He claimed to have been possessed by demons. Sellers was executed by lethal injection in 1999 at the Oklahoma State Penitentiary in McAlester, Oklahoma. For his last meal he had eggrolls, sweet and sour shrimp, and batter-fried shrimp. In 2010, Teresa Lewis became the first female convict to be killed by lethal injection in the state of Virginia. She was convicted of killing her husband and stepson. For her last meal she had sweet peas with butter, fried chicken, chocolate cake, and Dr Pepper. Frank Spisak was a lunatic with a Hitler toothbrush mustache who committed three racially motivated murders in 1982. He was killed by lethal injection in Ohio in 2011. For his last meal before he was put to death he had spaghetti with light tomato sauce, tossed salad with Italian dressing, chocolate cake, coffee and root beer.

Chester Wicker was executed by lethal injection in 1986 for the rape and murder of Suzanne Knuth. Wicker's last meal must rank as one of the most straight forward and simple requests. He simply asked for lettuce and tomatoes. Gary Carl Simmons was executed by lethal injection in 2006 for the murder of Jeremy Wolfe. In contrast to Wicker, Simmons had a massive junk food binge as his last meal. He requested a Pizza Hut Supreme Deep Dish Pizza, 10 packs of Parmesan cheese, 10 packs of ranch dressing, a family-size bag of Nacho Cheese Doritos, 8 ounces of jalapeno nacho cheese, 4 ounces of sliced jalapeno peppers, 2 large strawberry milkshakes, two cherry cokes, one super-sized order of McDonald's fries with extra ketchup and mayo, and two pints of strawberry ice cream.

Rhonda Belle Martin was an Alabama waitress who confessed to poisoning to death several members of her family in 1956. She was killed in the electric chair that same year. For her last meal she had a hamburger, mashed potatoes, cinnamon rolls and coffee. David Alan Gore was an American serial killer who confessed to six murders in Vero Beach and Indian River County, Florida in the 1980s. Gore was executed by lethal injection in 2012. For his last meal, Gore had fried chicken, French fries, and butter pecan ice cream.

Gregory Paul Lawler was executed for shooting dead a police officer and seriously injuring another one in 1997. For his last meal he had French onion soup, asparagus, ribeye steak, a baked potato with soar cream, dinner rolls with butter, pistachio ice cream, strawberries, milk and apple juice.

Ricky Ray Rector was convicted for two counts of murder (which happened in 1981) and sentenced to death in Arkansas. For his last meal he had steak, fried chicken, cherry Kool-Aid and pecan pie. Russell Bucklew was convicted of first-degree murder, kidnapping and first-degree burglary in 1997. He had a smoked brisket sandwich, two portions of fries, a cola and a banana split for his last meal. Karla Faye Tucker was convicted of murder in Texas in 1984 and executed by lethal injection after 14 years on death row. She was convicted for killing two people with a pickaxe during a burglary. For her last meal, Tucker requested a banana, a peach, and a garden salad with ranch dressing. By the way, want to know what Saddam Hussein had for his last meal before he was executed? The dictator chose boiled chicken and rice and several cups of warm water mixed with honey.

Not all killers accept a last meal. Aileen Wuornos declined a last meal before her execution and asked for black coffee. She apparently had a burger earlier in the day though.

Ted Bundy also declined to have a last meal before his execution. He was given the standard prison breakfast instead but he did not eat any of this. Although alcohol is rarely permitted in last meal requests it would obviously be of help. John George Haigh was, as we have noted, a British serial killer known as The Acid Bath Murderer. He killed at least six people but (as ever with serial killers) the real body count might be higher. Before he was hung in 1949, Haigh requested (and received) a large brandy. This soothed his nerves more effectively than any amount of food might have done.

How Many Serial Killers Had Normal Jobs?

The answer to this question is most them. A serial killer could be working in the same office as you and you wouldn't know it. A study showed that the most common skilled serial killer occupation was Aircraft machinist/assembler. The most common unskilled serial killer occupation was General labourer. The FBI once said that the perfect occupation for a serial killer would be a long haul truck driver - which is fairly obvious. The FBI say that serial killers can be classified as 'organised' or 'disorganised'. The former have friends and family and are able to function in a normal social way. The latter are feral lone wolves with no connections. Organised serial killers will most likely have a normal job while disorganised serial killers will be more likely to live off the grid or be a drifter.

A large number of serial killers have served in the military. This is often a consequence of the era they lived in. The United States had the Vietnam draft and countries like Britain used to have national service. Most nations had a larger army in the past than they do today. It is estimated that around 7% of serial killers in America served in the military. Jeffrey Dahmer was a medic in the armed forces and stationed in West Germany. While he was there, two soldiers accused Dahmer of drugging and then raping them. Dahmer apparently got kicked out of the army because of his drinking problems. He was never destined to last very long in such a rigid sort of institution.

Dennis Nilsen served in the British Army Catering Corps and was a chef in 1st Battalion the Royal Fusiliers. Nilsen served eleven years in the army and reached the rank of corporal. Dead bodies were not new to Nilsen before he became a killer or joined the police. He saw dead bodies in Aden when he was in the army. Dennis Nilsen said that when he was in Aden (now part of Yemen) the situation was volatile and getting out of control. The only thing the factions there could agree on is that they should target the British Army. Nielsen left in the army in the end because he was gay. As he got older, he started to stand out like a sore thumb as an unmarried soldier. In those days it was obviously a lot more difficult to be gay in the armed forces.

In 2010, Colonel Russell Williams was apprehended in connection to two murders. Williams commanded CFB Trenton, Canada's largest military airbase. Although a decorated and respected officer and pilot, he had a secret life as a prowler and rapist who broke into homes to steal female underwear and - eventually - kill. Robert Yates, who killed 17 prostitutes in the 1990s, was a decorated National Guard helicopter pilot. Other killers who served in the armed forces include Gary Ridgway, David Berkowitz, Dean Corll, Dennis Rader, Randy Kraft, Arthur Shawcross, and John Christie. Christie served in World War I and suffered a gas attack (which is ironic given his later crimes!) that left him unable to speak above a whisper. William Bonin served in Vietnam as a machine gunner in helicopters. Joseph James DeAngelo was another serial killer with a military background. He spent two years in the navy.

Ted Bundy once worked as the Assistant Director of the Seattle Crime Prevention Advisory Commission. Bundy also worked for the Department of Emergency Services (DES). This (in what can only be described as darkly ironic) was a government agency that searched for missing women. David Berkowitz was, among other things, a taxi driver and postal worker. Peter Sutcliffe was a gravedigger and then a HGV driver. Donald Gaskins once worked for a travelling carnival. John Wayne Gacy's access to victims was facilitated by his position as a building contractor. He was constantly in contact with teenagers and young men looking for some temporary work. Gacy, as we noted in the previous chapter, previously ran a KFC franchise. Jeffrey Dahmer used to work at the Ambrosia Chocolate Factory.

The serial killer Randall Woodfield was once selected in the 17th 1974 Draft by the Green Bay Packers as a wide receiver. Randall Woodfield was an unlikely serial killer in terms of his social background. Not only was he once a promising American football player but his parents were wealthy and his sisters became a lawyer and doctor. To say that Woodfield was the black sheep of the family would be an understatement indeed. It is estimated that Woodfield committed 44 murders and 60 sexual assaults but the true figure could be much higher. Woodfield later became a bouncer in some bars.

John Christie, the infamous 'gas killer' of 10 Rillington Place, was a police constable during World War 2. Christie is far from being the only killer to have served in the police. Joseph James DeAngelo (aka The Golden State Killer) was a police officer in Auburn. Many at the time suspected a police officer was the killer because the killer seemed to be savvy when it came to forensic evidence and covering his tracks. DeAngelo was kicked out of the police in 1979 after he was caught shoplifting. He later became a mechanic. Mikhail Popkov was born in Angarsk, Russia, in 1964. He is known as The Werewolf or The Angarsk Maniac. He killed over seventy women (and that's probably a conservative estimate). Not much is known about Popkov's childhood but we do know that as a young man he got married and joined the police. He later worked as a security guard. Popkov managed to gain the trust of a number of his victims by wearing his police officer's uniform.

Gerard John Schaefer was a sheriff's deputy in Martin County, Florida. In 1972 he picked up two hitchhiking girls and tied them to a tree. The girls escaped before he could do anything and Schaefer claimed he was simply trying to teach them about the perils of hitchhiking! He was not believed and sentenced for false imprisonment. While on bail, he tortured, raped, and killed two teenagers. When the remains of the girls were found in the woods, Schaefer became a suspect because of his prior offence. The police searched his home and found disturbing fiction stories he had written about rape plus some personal items which belonged to girls who had gone missing. It is believed that he may have killed eight young women and teenagers in total. Schaefer was stabbed to death in prison in 1995.

Dennis Nilsen is another serial killer who served in the police. In 1972 Nilsen was posted to Wilsden Green Police Station and served as a beat bobby before he eventually decided that this wasn't the career for him. Dennis Nilsen said that when he joined the police he was disappointed to find that the camaraderie he experienced in the army was not in evidence. Although he made some arrests while he was in the police, Nilsen never had to physically restrain or tackle a criminal. When he was a police officer, Dennis Nilsen sometimes walked the beat at Willesden Green on his own. If you lived in that area at the time you might well have walked past PC Nilsen in the street.

It is sometimes reported that Nilsen was booted out of the police for sexual indecency in the morgue. There is no evidence for this claim though. When he was a police officer, Nilsen and other recruits had to visit the morgue very soon into their service to get them used to dead bodies. Nilsen, as we have noted earlier, was in his element but one recruit he went with actually fainted at the sight of autopsied bodies. When he was in the police, Nilsen also once found two men having sex in a car at night. He couldn't bring himself to arrest them or say anything and so just left them alone. Incidents like this made Nilsen realise that it would be very difficult for a gay man like himself to be a police officer.

Nilsen eventually became a civil servant after he dropped out of the police. He was a recruitment interviewer. When he inquired about a job at the local Jobcentre, Nilsen was hired on the spot because of his police and army record. Nilsen's specific duty at the Jobcentre was to help unskilled workers find employment. Nilsen took his position at the Jobcentre very seriously because he liked to think of himself as a champion of the underdog. Nilsen was the Acting Executive

Officer at the employment office on Denmark Street, Soho. Denmark Street was known as Tin-Pan Alley. A number of famous musical artists (like The Sex Pistols and David Bowie) recorded here. No one at the Jobcentres where Nilsen worked ever noticed anything especially dark or out of the ordinary about him.

The 1950s serial killer Harvey Glatman was a TV repair man. Andrei Chikatilo killed over 50 people (mostly children) in Ukraine from 1978 to 1990. Believe it or not, Chikatilo worked as a teacher in the early 1970s. Dennis Rader fitted security alarms for a living. He said many people had alarms fitted by him because of their fear of the BTK killer! Fred West was briefly an ice cream man. Richard Ramirez was once a porter at the Holiday Inn. Joel Rifkin had a landscape gardening business. Another landscape gardener was Yvan Keller. Keller is known in true crime circles as The Pillow Killer. Keller claimed to have killed 150 people but the real figure is of course impossible to know. What we do know is that he killed at least 23 people in France, Switzerland and Germany. Keller targeted and robbed elderly women.

John Wayne Gacy once worked for a shoe company. Edward Kemper worked for the Highway Department. Kemper tried to join the police but his height and weight (he was 6'9 and weighed nearly 300 pounds) prevented him from being accepted. Herb Baumeister, who killed over twenty people in he 80s and 90s, had a chain of thrift store businesses. Albert Fish worked as a house painter and chauffeur. Larry Eyler (aka The Highway Killer) was also a house painter. The sadistic and evil Dean Corll workd for the family candy company. Patrick Wayne Kearney (aka The Trash Bag Killer) worked as an engineer for Hughes Aircraft. Rodney Alcala once had a counselling job at a New Hampshire arts camp for children.

Anthony Hardy was a London serial killer known as The Camden Ripper. His background was unusual for a serial killer. He had a degree from Imperial College and was once the director of his own company. His mental health seemed to crumble later on though. He tried to strangle his wife and became an alcoholic. Robert Hansen funded his Alaska bakery by staging an insurance hoax. He pretended his house had been robbed. Hansen had worked in a bakery since he was a child. He is inevitably known as The Butcher Baker in true crime articles. Vlado Taneski was a Macedonian serial killer who brutally raped and murdered three women from 2005 to 2008. The odd thing about this case is that Taneski was a journalist who had actually written articles about the murders!

Steven (The Suffolk Strangler) Wright used to work on the QE2 and had a family. He didn't really fit any serial killer stereotype. Luis Garavito, who murdered hundreds of children, sold religious cards for a living. John George Haigh is another killer who worked as a chauffeur. Randy Kraft was known as The Scorecard Killer because he kept a tally of his victims in the fashion of a scoresheet. The strange thing about Kraft, as we noted earlier, is that he was intelligent and worked in technology and computers. Arthur Gary Bishop, who was killed by lethal injection in 1980 for the murder of a number of young boys, once worked as a missionary in the Philippines.

There have been, as we have already touched upon, a number of serial killers who either operate or work in the medical world. Charles Edmund Cullen was a New Jersey born male nurse who was discovered to have deliberately given dozens of patients lethal overdoses in a number of hospitals. He is believed to have done this for the first time in 1988 but he was only convicted in 2008. Cullen told prosecutors that he had sought to mitigate the suffering of patients but this evidence was thrown out because of the fact that many of these patients had no critical or terminal condition and would have recovered if he hadn't killed them. Cullen may have killed as many as forty patients. Cullen came under suspicion in some of the hospitals he worked in but somehow managed to survive investigations. Tragically, it is believed that the chronic shortage of nurses was the main reason why he kept being employed again.

Carol M. Bundy, one of the Sunset Strip Killers, was a vocational nurse at Valley Medical Centre in Van Nuys. Dana Sue Gray is a female serial killer from California. She worked as a nurse and killed three older women in a gated community in 1994. The ferocity of the attacks shocked the police. One victim was left with a knife sticking out of her neck and another was strangled with a telephone cord. The motivation of Dana Sue Gray was money. She was addicted to shopping and had run up debts. She was captured after she was caught shopping using a credit card that belonged to one of her victims. In 1998 she was sentenced to life in prison.

H.H. Holmes attended various colleges as a teenager and got booted out of one of these schools for theft. In 1882 he entered University of Michigan's Department of Medicine and Surgery and managed to graduate in the end. Holmes later confessed to the murder of a medical school colleague as part of an insurance scam. Donald Harvey is another of those 'Angel of Death' medical killers. He claimed to have killed nearly 90 people in the end although the true number is almost impossible to ever know. He worked as an orderly at hospitals and this enabled him to kill dozens of patients. Many of his victims were cardiac patients. His methods of murder were not limited to any one means. He turned off ventilators, used arsenic, suffocation, sabotaged catheters, and even injected people with hepatitis.

Are There Female Serial Killers?

It has been estimated that around 15% of serial killers are women. Psychologist Marissa Harrison concluded from her study that female serial killers were mostly motivated by material gain whereas male serial killers were mostly motivated by sexual urges. Female serial killers are generally more likely to know their victims. Female serial killers are also more likely to work in the medical profession in some capacity. Female serial killers are much less likely to have prior criminal convictions than male serial killers and this, one might argue, makes it harder to see them coming. Female killers are way more likely to use poison that their male counterparts and they generally tend to be less gruesome. There are though, as ever, exceptions to these general facts.

Female killers who bump off husbands are generally known as Black Widows. An awful lot of female killers have killed their husbands. Some crime authors think that female serial killers have not received half as much ink as their male counterparts. Because of this we sometimes forget just how many female killers there have been down the decades.

'They're often described as quiet killers,' wrote Discover Magazine of female serial killers. 'They typically don't butcher, nor torture. They prefer poison — in 50 percent of all cases — and smothering to conspicuous knives and guns. They also tend to kill at home or at work, drawing less attention than the random, far-flung sprees common among men. In a 2013 paper analysing the characteristics of female serial killers, sociologist Amanda Farrell wrote that they kill, on average, over longer stretches of time than their male counterparts.'

Maria Swanenburg was a Dutch serial killer who may have murdered as many as 90 people in the 1880s. Her official death tally stands at 27. She was poisoner who used arsenic to kill her victims. She was given life in prison and died in 1915. She was considered to be a good neighbour who liked to care for the sick and old people. Little did they know she was actually trying to kill everyone! Joanna Dennehy is a female serial killer who stabbed three men to death with a knife in England in 2013. These were brutal random attacks done in daylight with no apparent motivation. Dennehy pleaded guilty in court (despite the objections of her defence team). She is only the third woman in Britain to receive a full life tariff after Myra Hindley and Rose West. Joanna Dennehy was a shocking case not only for the ruthless barbarity of her attacks but also because she came from a normal family. She showed no remorse for her crimes.

Jasmine Richardson is one of the youngest serial killers. In Alberta, Canada, in 2006, she murdered her parents and stabbed her eight year-old brother to death. She was just twelve years-old at the time. Jasmine Richardson was heavily under the influence of her 23 year-old boyfriend Jeremy Steinke - a nutty character who claimed to be a werewolf. The motive for the murders was that Richardson was distraught that her family didn't approve of her relationship with Steinke. Of course they didn't approve. She was only 12! Steinke was deemed to be involved in the murders. Jasmine Richardson and Jeremy Steinke were both convicted for their crimes. Steinke received three life sentences but Jasmine Richardson, in a move that angered many Canadians, was released after ten years and given a new identity.

Susan Carson and Michael Carson were dubbed The San Francisco Witch Killers. They were responsible for three murders from 1981 to 1983. The couple, who were said to take vast quantities of mind-altering drugs, became convinced that it was their mission to kill those in thrall to witchcraft and the occult. They killed a young woman in their apartment by caving her head in with a saucepan, a farm worker (the Carsons had a farm) by strangulation, and a hitchhiker by shooting. When they were apprehended, the Carsons were found to have a hit list of 'evil' people they planned to kill. The list included celebrities like Ronald Reagan and Johnny Carson. Susan Carson and Michael Carson are still suspects in twelve other murders. They both received life in prison for their crimes.

Amelia Dyer became known as The Reading Baby Farmer and The Angel Maker for her horrendous crimes in Victorian England. Dyer worked as a 'baby farmer' - this involved looking after illegitimate babies in the hope that someone might adopt them one day. Dyer deduced though that she could keep all the money she was paid to do this for herself if she just killed the babies and didn't have to spend money on food, clothes, medicine, and bedding. It is estimated that she killed 400 babies. Their bodies started to be found in the Thames and Dyer was arrested in 1896. Dyer's defence team pleaded insanity on her behalf but nonetheless she was executed for her unforgivable crimes. 57 year-old Amelia Dyer was hung at Newgate Gaol. Amelia Dyer is considered to be one of the coldest and most evil killers in history. She literally had a lump of coal for a heart.

Mary Bell is often cited as one of the youngest serial killers. She was ten when she strangled two toddlers in the English city of Newcastle in 1968. It is debatable that two murders made Mary Bell a serial killer but most experts believe she would almost certainly have killed again if she hadn't been caught. Mary Bell had some of the traits we associate with serial killers. She seemed to enjoy the attention the murders brought to her area and even left a cryptic (if childish) confession note in a local nursery. Mary, who was manipulative and intelligent, also tried to pin the deaths on her best friend Norma. Mary Bell was released from prison in her early twenties. She later got married and had a child.

Rose West claimed to be innocent but this was never credible. She was actually vital in allowing Fred West to pick up a number of victims. The presence of a wife made him seem like a normal (as far as the werewolf like Fred West could ever appear normal) person rather than a conspicuous threat. It was proven that Charmaine, the daughter of Fred and Rose, was murdered while Fred West was in prison. Rose West is believed to have killed more than one person and was clearly an accomplice. There were bodies under the patio and in the cellar at 25 Cromwell Street so it seems risible to think Rose West knew nothing of this. The children of Fred and Rose West have said they were sometimes asked to hide in a box while their parents did something in secret. That secret something is assumed to have been moving and disposing of bodies.

Aileen Wuornos is arguably the most famous female serial killer. She killed seven men in total from 1989 to 1990. Aileen Wuornos worked as a prostitute and picked up her victims on the I-75 highway. She would target middle-aged men in nice cars. Wuornos would start to undress in the car and ask the driver to pull over somewhere secluded. Then she would get out of the car and shoot them before stealing their wallets. Wuornos would often shoot her victims multiple times. Her motivation for the murders was that she wanted to support her girlfriend Ty. Ian Brady and Myra Hindley became known as The Moors Murderers for abducting and killing five children on Saddleworth Moor between 1963 and 1965. The crimes shocked Britain and still haunt the city of Manchester. The Moors Murders shocked Britain most of all because a woman was involved. There were attempts, especially by Lord Longford, to release Myra Hindley from prison but he newspapers and British public were appalled by this. Hindley died in prison in 2002.

The most prolific female serial killer was Elizabeth Báthory, who practised vampirism on girls and young women. She is alleged to have killed hundreds virgins in order to drink their blood and bathe in it. Juana Barraza was known as The Old Lady Killer. She murdered between 42 and 48 elderly woman before being captured in 2006. Dorothea Puente ran a boarding house in Sacramento that housed elderly and mentally handicapped boarders. Puente would murder them so that she could steal their social security money. She was convicted of nine murders. Judy Buenoano was known as The Black Widow. She poisoned her husband, drowned her son, and tried to kill her lover with a bomb! She went to the electric chair in 1998. Nannie Doss, who was born in 1905, was nicknamed the Giggling Granny because talking about her murders amused her. Doss killed eleven people and all of them were related to her.

Belle Gunness was a Norweigian woman who moved to the United states in the late 19th century. She had a farm in Indiana but any men who went to this farm were seemingly never seen again. Belle Gunness put an ad in the paper looking for a husband but this was one ad you didn't want to respond to. Her life and death is still shrouded in some mystery. In 1908 the farm burned down and the police found the remains of eleven victims - which included Belle's children and a woman's head. Did Belle die in the blaze or did she stage the whole thing to escape? The jury is still out. Leonarda Cianciulli, the Italian woman who turned her victims into cakes and soap, murdered Virginia Cacioppo, a former soprano. Cianciulli said she almost decapitated Virginia Cacioppo by striking her with an axe.

Tracey Wiggington is an Australian murderer who is known as The Lesbian Vampire Killer as she was a self styled vampire who killed a man in order to drink his blood. She was involved in killing a man named Edward Baldock. The stabbing was so violent and frenzied that Baldock's head was nearly severed. Wigginton told the police - "I walked around behind him, I took my knife out of my back pocket, he asked me what I was doing, I said nothing and stabbed him. He went up to grab my hand. I pushed his hand down, withdrew the knife, and stabbed him in the side of the neck, I stabbed him in the other side of the neck, and I continuously stabbed him. I then grabbed him by the hair on his head and pulled back, stabbed him in the front of the throat and at that stage he was still alive."

Clementine Barnabet was born in St. Martinville, Louisiana in 1894. Banabet was supposedly the priestess of a cult group called The Church of Sacrifice. You can probably guess what this nutty cult group believed in. The clue is in the title. Her family moved to Lafayette around the turn of the century and were all involved in this cult. In 1911, led by Clementine, the cult slaughtered some families by barging into their homes. The method of murder was an axe - which naturally made these killings incredibly brutal and bloody. Amy Archer-Gilligan, who worked at a nursing home in Connecticut in the early 1900s, murdered dozens of patients to get her hands on their life insurance policies. Beverley Allitt was a British nurse convicted of murdering four children with insulin. She was given life in prison in 1993.

There are many more female killers out there and they come from all backgrounds and all nations. While there are not as many female serial killers as male ones they can be just as deadly and just as dangerous. In fact, one might argue that, in many cases, female serial killers have a cunning and nous that their male counterparts don't always seem to possess.

Do Serial Killers Get Married And Have Families?

Yes, even serial killers even get married and have children. And all serial killers obviously have relatives and some sort of family. It is sometimes surprising how many serial killers have wives, children, and girlfriends who are unaware of their true nature. The ability of serial killers to appear normal to those around them has been described as the 'mask of sanity'. Herb Baumeister was a store owner from Indiana who was married with children. In the early 1990s, the police in the area where Baumeister lived were investigating the disappearance of a number of gay men. They got a tip that Baumeister might be a link in the mystery and went to his isolated house at Fox Hollow Farm. There turned out to be eleven bodies buried on the property. Baumeister fled to Canada and promptly shot himself. Baumeister's wife didn't even know he was gay let alone a serial killer!

Ted Bundy met a single mother named Elizabeth Kloepfer in 1969 and they had an on/off relationship that ran to 1976. Kloepfer later wrote a book about her life with Bundy. She loved Bundy and wanted to marry him. At first she thought the police suspicion of him was ridiculous but - gradually - she began to have doubts. Ted Bundy was always kind to Elizabeth Kloepfer's daughter. He would sing her lullabies at night. When she found out that her boyfriend Ted Bundy was a serial killer, Elizabeth Kloepfer asked him if he had ever been tempted to kill her. Bundy said that he had thought about it once but would never have gone through with it.

Bundy later married a woman named Carole Ann Boone in bizarre circumstances. Ted Bundy and Carole Ann Boone met when they both worked at the Washington State Department of Emergency Services (DES) in Olympia, Washington. At his last trial in Orlando, Ted Bundy put Carole Ann Boone on the stand and proposed marriage to her (which she accepted).

Carole Ann Boone was a deluded woman who, contrary to all evidence, refused to believe that Bundy was a serial killer. Ted Bundy and Carole Ann Boone actually had a child together in Bundy's last years. The daughter of Ted Bundy and Carole Ann Boone was the result of a conjugal visit to prison. The prison guards were bribed. It is not really known what happened to Ted Bundy's daughter with Carole Ann Bone. There have been newspaper reports that she moved to England and got married.

Very little is known about Ted Bundy's siblings. During his trial for the Carol DeRonch abduction, Bundy's sister Linda had a statement read out in court. The statement by Linda insisted that her brother Ted was a very nice man who would never hurt anyone. Ted Bundy's mother also refused to believe he was a serial killer. She called him the 'greatest son in the world' - even as Bundy was in court on multiple murder and abduction charges. This shock and denial is not uncommon when it comes to the relatives of serial killers.

The relatives of John Norman Collins refused to believe he as a serial killer - despite the considerable weight of evidence which suggested otherwise. Serial killers are obviously at their best when with relatives or friends. They can seem kind and decent. Their depraved and evil secret lives are hidden from the world. Only their victims see their true nature.

Dennis Rader's daughter said the family never suspected that he was a serial killer. She said they obviously would have gone straight to the police if they had any suspicions. Rader walked his daughter down the aisle when she got married. When he was arrested, Rader's wife Paula Dietz told the police that Dennis was a great father who would never hurt anyone. She was absolutely bewildered to discover that her placid husband was an evil killer. Despite the fact that he was gay, John Wayne Gacy was twice married with children. The two obvious theories are that he was afraid to 'come out' and used his family as cover for his sadistic secret life. Gacy's second wife Paula Dietz eventually left him when she kept finding gay nude magazines in the house.

One of the strangest things about the disturbing life of Albert Fish is that he got married and had six children. There were never any accounts of Fish abusing or harming his children. He was said to be a good father. Gary Ridgeway, as we have noted, didn't kill for ten years after meeting his last wife. He was happily married when he was captured. Ridgeway's wife Judith Mawson later wrote a book about her awful experience of finding out her husband was a killer. She said that she would find it almost impossible ever to trust a man again. Robert Lee Yates was married all the while he was murdering women. "How could I not see the signs?" the wife of Yates said when he was arrested. "Especially when he said he was going hunting, and he was dressed up nice and had cologne on. You don't go out hunting with cologne on. But, see, you're so close to somebody you don't see it."

The mass poisoner Jane Toppan was jilted at the alter - which may well have been the main source of her anger and mental instability. Toppan said that if she had become a wife and mother she never would have killed. Joseph James DeAngelo married an attorney and had three daughters. The wife of Peter Sutcliffe actually stayed married to him a long time even after it was revealed that he was the Yorkshire Ripper. By all accounts she was not the full shilling herself. The address of the Yorkshire Ripper (aka Peter Sutcliffe) was 6 Garden Lane, Bradford. Believe it or not, his former wife still lives in this house. Arthur Shawcross was married four times. Donald Henry Gaskins was married five times and had two children. Colin Ireland was married twice. Albert DeSalvo (aka The Boston Strangler) was married with two children. Dorothea Puente was married twice.

The wife of Harold Shipman (the British doctor who murdered hundreds of his patients) stood by him during his trial and conviction and maintained that he was innocent. Mrs Shipman simply refused to believe that her dear old Harold could have killed anyone on purpose. John Christie was another serial killer who was married although (as you might expect) this didn't turn out so well. Christie throttled his wife Ethel in 1952 so that he could plunder her bank account. His motives for murder were sometimes sexual and sometimes financial. Nannie Doss was married several times but - of course - always careful to make sure her husbands had a life insurance policy. Perhaps the strangest part of The Toy-Box murders is that David Parker Ray's daughter Jesse was an accomplice. She and a woman named Cindy Hendy helped Parker find victims. A man named Dennis Yancy was also an accomplice.

Fritz Haarmann got married despite being (secretly) gay. The medical killer Charles Edmund Cullen was married. Serhiy Tkach (aka The Pavlohrad Maniac) was married four times and had children. Patrick Wayne Kearney got married as a young man but it didn't last very long. Andrei Chikatilo, who killed over fifty children and young people, was married and had two children. His wife later said - "If I had known what my husband was doing all those years, then, of course, I would have done something to stop him. But how was I to know?" Leonard Lake's first marriage apparently collapsed because his wife found out he was making porno bondage movies in his spare time. Lake moved to Northern California and lived a hippie commune sort of life (obviously without the peace and love though in the end). He married a woman who had no qualms abut his porno bondage films. Quite the contrary. She was happy to star in them.

Bill Lee Suff was born in California in 1950. Suff mutilated and killed around twelve sex workers in Riverside County from 1989 to 1991. He tends to be known in true crime circles as The Riverside Prostitute Killer or The Lake Elsinore Killer. In 1974, Suff and his wife were accused of causing the death of their baby daughter in Texas by administering a beating. Suff's wife was cleared of the charges but he was convicted and given a sentence of 70 years in prison. The baby was found to have a number of broken bones and the autopsy revealed the child had been killed by a heavy blow to the abdomen. In 1991 Suff's new 3-month-old baby daughter, Bridgette, was removed by

San Bernardino County authorities after the child sustained suspicious injuries. Suff was not only a danger to women but also his own children.

Amelia Dyer was married when she was younger but struggled financially when her husband died. Tragically, this might have been a factor in her 'baby farming' murders. Mikhail Popkov was born in Angarsk, Russia, in 1964. He is known as The Werewolf or The Angarsk Maniac. He killed over seventy women (and that's probably a conservative estimate). Popkov was apparently tilted into madness by an adulterous wife. This seemed to trigger an obsessive and evil quest to extract revenge against women. Strangely, his wife Elena Popkov continued to support him though and said he was innocent!

Even the worst serial killers have had wives, girlfriends, and even children. They often have supportive mothers. It is often difficult for relatives of serial killers to accept that the person they have known for many years and in many cases lived with was not the person they thought. This results in a lot of denial but in many cases the relatives of serial killers accept what has happened and simply feel disgusted. A case in point is William Bonin. The family of Bonin ignored the request to claim his remains from San Quentin State Prison after he was executed. They just wanted to forget he ever existed.

Who Was The Most Prolific Serial Killer?

One of the grim things about the most prolific serial killers is that in many cases they tend to be child killers. In places like South America, India, and Pakistan literally hundreds of street children can be killed without anyone apparently deducing that a serial killer is at large. The South American killer Pedro López is known as The Monster of the Andes. He is generally regarded to be perhaps the most prolific serial killer of all and claims to have committed 350 murders. All of his victims were children. The Colombian serial killer Luis Garavito, who first became active in the early 1990s, might have killed as many as 300 children. All of his victims were under 16.

Javed Iqbal was born in Lahore, Pakistan, in 1956. Iqbal is regarded to be the worst serial killer in the history of Pakistan. A lot of his victims were orphans and homeless street kids. After he put the remains in vats of acid he would dump the containers in the river. Iqbal is estimated to have killed over a hundred people. Daniel Camargo Barbosa was born in Colombia in 1930. He is believed to have raped and murdered well over one hundred young girls. In 1994, the 67 year-old Daniel Camargo Barbosa was stabbed to death in prison by Geovanny Noguera. Noguera was a relative of one of Barbosa's victims and took his chance to extract revenge for the family.

Harold Shipman was a GP in Manchester who murdered (at least) 218 of his patients with injections of diamorphine (heroin) from 1975 to 1998. The body count is so high that we might never know just how many people Shipman killed. It is possible that Shipman's true kill count might be pushing 300. When it comes to medical professionals, Miyuki Ishikawa is up there with the worst killers. Ishikawa killed more than 103 newborn children in Japan in the post-war years. Niels Högel was a German nurse who killed at least eighty patients in 1999 and 2000. Högel might well have killed hundreds more people.

The most prolific serial killer in the United States could well be Samuel Little. Little claims to have murdered 93 women from 1970 to 2005. The police believe he is not lying and have verified up to 50 victims so far. Little's method of murder was nearly always strangulation. Yang Xinhai was born in China in 1968. He is the most prolific Chinese serial killer since the establishment of the People's Republic of China. It is believed that around 25 of an estimated 67 victims were also raped by Xinhai. There were never any survivors of these attacks and entire families were slaughtered. Kampatimar Shankariya was a killer in India who murdered at least seventy people with a hammer in 1977 and 1978. Very little is known about this killer because the Indian authorities did not allow the media to openly cover the case.

In terms of verified victims, Mikhail Popkov is certainly up among the worst serial killers with 83+ victims. Rodney Alcala was a brutal serial killer active in the 1970s. Alcala was very adept at leaving no forensic evidence. He would lure girls for a photography session and then murder them. The police found hundreds of photographs of these girls but finding the bodies and remains was another matter entirely. One salient reason why Rodney Alcala went undetected for so long was that he moved around a lot. There were sometimes large geographical spaces between his victims and this obviously made it much more difficult to establish any pattern. For all we know, Alcala might have murdered more than a hundred people.

Pedro Rodrigues Filho was born in Brazil in 1954. He tends to be known as Pedrinho Matador (Killer Petey) or The Brazilian Dexter. He got the later name because a large number of his victims were criminals and pretty awful people themselves. It's slightly uncertain if Filho was a serial killer or just a violent gangster. He tended to blur the lines between these two categories at the best of times. Filho, as twisted as it was, did have a sort of code where he only killed criminals or those he felt had wronged him. In this sense then he is not quite what you would call a 'pure' serial killer. Filho killed over one hundred people - including murders in prison.

Gary Ridgway and Ted Bundy are generally regarded to be the second and third most prolific American killers but this is based on verified victims. We simply don't know how many people they really killed. Bundy is believed to have held back a lot of information about his murders. Even when he was on death row and had become confessional in a bid to evade the electric chair (darkly dubbed his 'bones for time' policy) Bundy said that there were murders he would never talk about because they were too 'close' to home. What he is presumed to have meant by this is that he did some murders that he didn't want to talk about because they involved very young victims or people he knew.

Only one of Bundy's verified victims was a child so it was not his usual MO. If Bundy did kill other children he obviously didn't want to talk about it. So, we don't really know how many people Bundy and Ridgeway really killed. They could have killed hundreds. The verified figures are 49 for Ridgeway and 35 for Bundy. In the end then it is difficult to establish precise facts for how many people a lot of serial killers really killed. Not all serial killers tell the truth. Some even exaggerate how many murders they conducted in an attempt to make themselves more infamous. We generally know though who the very worst killers (in terms of numbers) were and, sadly, they tend to be those awful and notorious child killers in South America.

Were There Famous Serial Killers Who Were Never Caught?

There are of course a lot of serial killers who were never caught. In cases where serial killers were never caught, the most obvious suspects naturally become people who died or were incarcerated around the time the murders stopped. The Long Island Killer was the name given to a serial killer who is believed to have been active in the Long Island area for twenty years. His last victim was found in 2013. Because this killer was able (so far at least) to evade capture or identification, the police believe he might possibly have worked in law enforcement himself (something which, as we have seen in previous chapters, is far from unheard of when it comes to serial killers). The Long Island Killer is clearly very savvy and clever when it comes to not leaving any incriminating evidence in his (or her?) wake.

The Axeman of New Orleans was an American serial killer active in New Orleans, Louisiana, in 1918 and 1919. There were six people killed and six injured during his bloody spree of violence. The killer was never identified and seemed to target the local Italian community. The killer used an axe or razor to kill the victims. The victims were mostly female but he killed a few men who were unfortunate enough to be in the houses he had broken into. Sexual sadism was the most likely motive as the killer never seemed to rob the victims. Because the victims were Italian-Americans some sort of Mafia link was suspected but this was never proven. The identity of the killer remains a mystery.

Zodiac was the name given to a killer who operated in California in the 60s and 70s. The killer, who was never found, claimed to have killed thirty people. The police still periodically re-open the case if fresh information comes to light. The Zodiac Killer targeted couples who were parked up in cars. He would shoot both the man and woman. This suggested that he was an outcast in society and was embittered and angered by seeing couples in love. Interestingly, Zodiac seemed to be something of a weekend killer so probably had a job. The killer began contacting newspapers in 1969 and identified himself as Zodiac. He was clearly eager to enjoy his moment in the spotlight. The killer wrote a number of letters which he said contained codes and ciphers which - if cracked - would reveal his identity. Although some of these codes have been cracked though so far they haven't actually revealed the true identity of the killer.

The Monster of Florence was a killer who murdered around sixteen people in Italy from 1968 to 1985. The killer had an MO very similar to the Zodiac Killer in America. The Monster of Florence would shoot couples who were sitting together in a car. The killer sometimes removed the sex organs of his female victims. The 1999 novel Hannibal was inspired by the Florence case. The killer was never caught by the Italian police although theories continue to abound. One such theory is that a satanic cult was behind the murders. The Thames Torso Murders was a series of unsolved murders which occurred in London from 1887 to 1889. There were four female victims in all and they were found floating in the Thames. The victims had legs and arms cut off and were often (as the name of the killer implies) just a torso. There was some mutilation of the stomachs. The police did not link these murders into the Jack the Ripper case because they felt the MO was too different.

Hammersmith in London was the scene of a number of murders in 1964 and 1965. The killer became known as Jack the Stripper because the murder victims were prostitutes. However, despite a huge police operation, the killer was never found and the murders remain a mystery. One of the more outlandish and bizarre theories (which, believe it or not, has even been the basis of a book) is that the killer was the world champion boxer turned actor Freddie Mills. The victims were nearly all in their twenties and are believed to have been killed in private before their bodies were dumped in a public place. Chief Superintendent John Du Rose was in charge of the investigation for Scotland Yard and had six-hundred police officers involved in the search for Jack the Stripper. They set up observation posts in a 24 square mile area of London and questioned thousands of potential suspects and yet - remarkably - they never found the killer.

The Texarkana Moonlight Murders featured an unknown killer who seemed to have stepped straight out of a real life horror film. 'Texarkana, a small town that straddles the state line between Texas and Arkansas, is also known as The Town That Dreaded Sundown, thanks to the 1976 horror flick of the same name,' wrote the Line-Up. 'Set in Texarkana and based loosely on a string of local slayings, the proto-slasher film came out just two years after The Texas Chain Saw Massacre and Black Christmas, and two years before Halloween. Yet the true story behind the Texarkana Moonlight Murders is as chilling as anything seen on the silver screen—and made all the more unsettling because the case remains unsolved nearly 70 years later. The mysterious Moonlight Murders rocked the sleepy southern town of Texarkana in 1946. Police on either side of the state line struggled to work as one while the killings themselves possessed the iconic quality of urban legend. Young couples parked at the end of a lonely country road, savaged after the sun went down.

'In fact, some claim that the infamous campfire tale of lovers who catch a report of a hook-handed killer on the car radio only to discover a bloody hook hanging from their back door can be traced to the Texarkana Moonlight Murders. The killer, described by witnesses as wearing a white mask or sack with holes cut for eyes, was dubbed the Phantom Killer or Phantom Slayer—a name that, like so much about the case, seemed ready-made for drive-in theaters. While the Phantom was on the loose, Texarkana was like a city under siege. Residents armed themselves and curfews were set for local businesses. In spite of the involvement of the Texas Rangers, no conclusive arrest was ever made in connection with the Moonlight Murders.

'Theories spread wildly about the Phantom Killer's identity. The killer's targeting of couples and lack of other identifiable motives, such as burglary or revenge, led many in the area to believe that the killer was some sort of "sex maniac". Nearly 400 people were arrested in connection with the killings. Suspects included a University of Arkansas freshman who committed suicide in 1948, an escaped German prisoner of war, and an L.A. resident who believed that he may have committed the crimes while in a coma. Many people believe that local man named Youell Swinney—arrested in 1947 for auto theft—was the Phantom. His wife confessed to as much at the time, but by law she could not testify against her husband. She later repudiated her confession. Swinney remained in prison as a habitual offender until 1973, and died in 1994, without ever implicating himself in the murders.'

The Atlanta Ripper was a killer who is believed to have killed around fifteen (and probably) more women in Atlanta in 1911 and 1912. However, this killer was never captured or identified. All the victims were young black women and the killer had a grisly habit of slashing the throats of his targets. The killer had a rather strange habit too of removing the clothes of the victim and then stacking them in a neat bundle next to the body. Emma Lou Sharp, who survived an encounter with the killer, described him as a tall dark skinned man who wore a black hat. The killer was very brutal. One victim was nearly decapitated and another had part of her skull crushed. A coupling pin from a train was used to bludgeon one victim. It is said that the Ripper cut the heart out of another victim and left it by the body.

The Belize Ripper was an unidentified Belizean serial killer responsible for the abduction, rape and murder of five girls in Belize between 1998 and 2000. No one was ever convicted of these murders. The Belize Ripper suspects included an American serial killer named Lonnie David Franklin Jr who had connections to the country. The Butcher of Mons was the name given to a Belgian serial killer who committed five murders in 1996 and 1997. The victims (all female) were expertly dismembered and left in plastic bags by an embankment. The identity of The Butcher of Mons was never established. In the seventies and eighties the remains of several boys were found in sewers in the Frankfurt Rhine-Main area of Germany. The victims were bound and many of them were rent boys or drug users (they were the usual type of vulnerable victims that serial killers target). Although they had some suspects the German police were never able to convict anyone of the sewer murders.

The Doodler was the name given to a serial killer who killed at least five men in San Francisco in 1974 and 1975. The victims, who were all gay, were usually picked up in bars. The killer got his name because he would 'doodle' a sketch of the victim as they chatted in a bar. The victims found this quite charming and it obviously lulled them into what can only be described as a false sense of security (to say the least). The killer was described as an urbane young black man but he was never arrested and to this day his true identity remains unknown. It is believed that the police actually questioned a man they suspected of being The Doodler in 1976. This man was never named in public and it seems the police simply didn't have enough evidence to charge him with anything. As a consequence, the identity of The Doodler remained an elusive mystery.

The Frankford Slasher was a serial killer who operated in and around the neighborhood of Frankford in Philadelphia, Pennsylvania from 1985 to 1990. Around nine women were raped and stabbed to death. A man was convicted for one of these murders but he could not be connected to the others - which left them to remain a mystery. The Sleepy Hollow Killer is the name of an unidentified South African rapist and serial killer responsible for the rapes and murders of at least 13 women around Pietermaritzburg and the Midlands of KwaZulu-Natal. The Sleepy Hollow Killer was never caught. The Connecticut River Valley Killer gruesomely stabbed to death at least seven women in and around Claremont, New Hampshire and the Connecticut River Valley in the 1980s. The

Connecticut River Valley Killer was also never captured.

The Alphabet Murders are an unsolved series of child murders which occurred between 1971 and 1973 in Rochester, New York. 'The Alphabet Killer is considered to be one of the greatest unsolved mysteries as far as crime is concerned in the United States,' wrote the Greatest Unsolved Mysteries website. 'The individual that committed what is referred to as the Alphabet Murders have perplexed law enforcement officials in the area of Rochester, New York since the year of 1971. Three very young females were taken by the killer, violently raped, and then murdered immediately thereafter. What makes this case particularly interesting when it comes to the investigation is that all the three children had names in which their first name and their last name had the exact same initial.

'Each girl's first and last name started with the same letter. Each child was ten years old. Each child was discovered in a city that started with the same letter as their name. Each child was from a Catholic family. Each child lived in a poverty stricken home. Each child suffered from either disciplinary and/or academic challenges at school. Due to the fact that each of the victims of the alphabet murders had these things in common, it was believed that the killer likely worked with a social service group. Many even thought that they could have known the families, or that they worked at the school where the children attended. While several suspects were interviewed the case remains "cold". The alphabet killer may still reside among us.'

The Eastbound Strangler is an unidentified serial killer responsible for the murders of four women near Atlantic City, New Jersey in 2006. Despite a police investigation and reward fund appealing for information, the killer has yet to be captured. The I-70 killer is an unidentified American serial killer who is known to have killed six store clerks in the Midwest in the spring of 1992. The victims were shot and had their stores robbed. Although the police were able to use eyewitnesses to get a sense of what the killer looked like no one was ever convicted of the murders. The Saw-Killer of Hanover was responsible for four murders in Germany in the 1970s. The victims usually had their bodies sawn in half or their limbs cut off. However, none of the victims could be identified and this made capturing the killer even more difficult. Although similar grisly murders have occasionally happened in Germany in later decades no one has ever been connected to the 1970s killings or convicted for the crimes.

The Skid Row Stabber is an unidentified American serial killer responsible for the murders of 11 people in the Los Angeles neighborhood known as Skid Row in the 1970s. The victims were (as the name implies) stabbed to death. Bobby Joe Maxwell was originally convicted of the crimes but later evidence cast doubt on this. As a consequence, The Skid Row Stabber might still be at large. The Denver Strangler was an unidentified serial killer operating in Denver, Colorado from 1894 to 1903. The Strangler killed three prostitutes but no one was ever convicted of the crimes. The Redhead Murders was a case where around ten women were killed between 1978 and 1992 in Tennessee, Arkansas, Kentucky, Mississippi, Pennsylvania, and West Virginia. The common link was that the victims all had red hair. The killer responsible for the Redhead Murders has yet to be caught.

The Cleveland Torso Murderer is one of the grisliest serial killers never captured. 'What's more terrifying than a serial killer?' wrote Film Daily. 'One that was never, ever caught. In the history of serial killers in the US, it's amazing that the Cleveland Torso Murderer is not often talked about. From 1935-38, this unknown killer terrorized the city of Cleveland, targeting those in vulnerable circumstances, and left between 12-20 people dead. Even outsmarted famed lawman Eliot Ness, leaving a black mark on his distinguished record. The Murderer was very deliberate in picking his victims. They were either working poor, drifters, or homeless. The Murderer did not show gender preference toward his victims. He killed both men and women. The bodies always ended up the same way: beheaded, dismembered, and disposed of. A lot of the male victims were castrated as well. In addition, some of the victims showed signs of a chemical treatment being applied to the bodies. This was still a time when forensic science was in a relative infancy, so not a lot could be gleaned from that. Even worse, the Murderer disposed of the bodies well. Many of his victims weren't found until some time after their deaths had passed.

'Like Jack the Ripper, the Cleveland Torso Murderer had canonical victims and non-canonical but likely victims. There are 12 canonical murders associated with the Murderer, most of them have never been identified. In addition to the canonical murders, police believe that the killer likely had 20 victims in total. There are two arrests in the case of the Cleveland Torso Murderer. One of the suspects arrested is believed to be more likely than the other. Or, at least, Ness believed that this suspect, Dr. Francis Sweeney, was the Murderer. Sweeney was a medical soldier in WWI, where he performed field amputations. The second arrest goes to Frank Dolezal, who had a connection to the eighth victim Florence Polillo. Police were desperate for arrest. So they arrest Dolezal, beat a confession out of him (which he retracted), and, then, Dolezal mysteriously died while in custody. He was officially cleared decades later. The final theory associated with the case is that, like Jack the Ripper, the Cleveland Torso Murderer is actually multiple killers, who heard about the deaths and copied each other in order to make it look like a serial killer.'

The Freeway Phantom was serial killer who was active in Washington, D.C. from April 1971 through to September 1972. The Phantom strangled, raped, and killed six women but he was never caught. The Flat-Tire murders were five connected, unsolved murders in Dade County, Florida in 1975. The killer in the Flat-Tire murders is believed to have let air out of his victims cars and then offered them assistance on the road before killing them. These were brutal murders (some of the victims were injured so badly they couldn't be identified) and the killer was clearly very cunning. Ted Bundy is sometimes cited as a possible suspect in the Flat-Tire murders although he denied this accusation.

Bible John is an unidentified serial killer who is believed to have murdered three young women between 1968 and 1969 in Glasgow. Bible John is believed to have met the victims at the Barrowland Ballroom. Some criminologists believe that the convicted murderer Peter Tobin might have been Bible John. There are many more mysterious serial killers who were never captured. The most famous of all of these is of course Jack the Ripper. Jack the Ripper murdered and dismembered five women in the Whitechapel district of London in brutal fashion. However, he was never caught and we still don't know who he really was. The Ripper targeted prostitutes and left some hideously gruesome crime scenes. He hacked out internal organs and disfigured the faces of his unfortunate victims.

During the Jack the Ripper murders, Queen Victoria received thousands of letters from women demanding that the police do more to catch the killer. The victims were Mary Ann Nichols, Annie Chapman, Elizabeth Stride, Catherine Eddowes, and Mary Jane Kelly. Ripper suspects include Montague John Druitt, Seweryn Klosowski, Aaron Kosminski, Michael Ostrog, John Pizer, James Thomas Sadler, Francis Tumblety, William Henry Bury, Thomas Neill Cream, Thomas Hayne Cutbush, Frederick Bailey Deeming, Walter Sickert, James Maybrick, Charles Allen Lechmere, and James kelly.

One of the first books inspired by Jack the Ripper was The Mystery of Jack the Ripper by Leonard Matters. The book suggested that the Ripper was a doctor who became enraged after his son was killed by a dose of syphilis he'd caught from a prostitute. In 1923, William Tufnell LeQuex wrote a book in which he suggested Jack the Ripper was a Russian doctor involved in a Czarist plot to murder women in London and make the British police and establishment seem weak and ineffective. The barrister and teacher Montague John Druitt is a frequent Ripper suspect because he was found floating in the Thames (presumably a suicide) not long after the last Ripper murder. There is no firm evidence though that the Oxford educated Ruitt was the Ripper.

Walter Sickert is a recurring Jack the Ripper suspect. This is perhaps inevitable as a consequence of his strange paintings and the fact that he was apparently fond of sharing lurid Ripper tales at parties. The crime writer Patricia Cornwell wrote a book in which she argued that Walter Sickert was Jack the Ripper. The general consensus is that Patricia Cornwell's insistence that Jack the Ripper was Walter Sickert doesn't really hold water. She claims, for example, that Sickert was angered by his impotence. However, we know that Sickert committed adultery on his wife, had many mistresses, and once had a child out of wedlock.

William Withey Gull, physician-in-ordinary to Queen Victoria, is often lumped in with Ripper suspects. This is a blurring of fiction with fact. Gull has been portrayed as responsible for the murders in a number of works of Ripper fiction (most famously perhaps the brilliant graphic novel From Hell by Alan Moore) but in reality was an old man recovering from a heart attack at the time of the murders. Stephen Knight's book Jack the Ripper: The Final Solution is responsible for the Jack the Ripper conspiracy that has Prince Albert Edward Victor and Royal Physician Sir William Gull plus a Freemason conspiracy all involved in the Whitechapel murders. Knight's book is entertaining but more fiction than fact. Stephen Knight's Royal and Masonic conspiracy theory concerning Jack the Ripper was the basis not only of Alan Moore's From Hell but also the 1988 Jack the Ripper TV miniseries with Michael Caine. Some have suggested that the killing of Mary Kelly by Jack the Ripper was suggestive of Masonic rituals in the way the heart was burned.

During the search for Jack the Ripper, the police investigated a number of medical students because of the theory that the killer had some medical knowledge. However, this turned up no leads or suspects. A recent FBI profile of Jack the Ripper dismissed the theory that the Ripper had medical knowledge.

They judged him to be a shabby loner and not someone of high society or any standing. Many believe that Jack the Ripper was much more likely to have been a butcher than someone with medical knowledge. During the Jack the Ripper murders, prostitutes reported the activities of a creepy man who always threatened to 'cut' them up. He was known simply as Leather Apron. One of the reasons why there were so few eye (and ear!) witnesses to Jack the Ripper's murders is that sewage at that time was left to fester in the street and cellars. People usually closed their windows to block out the stench.

Speculative female Jack the Ripper suspects include Mary Pearcey, who killed her lover's wife and child, and Constance Kent, who murdered her brother. The evidence though in both cases is vague at best. William Stewart's 1939 book on Jack the Ripper suggested that the Ripper might have been a midwife. When the poisoner Thomas Nell Cream was hanged in 1892, he claimed - with his dying words - to have been Jack the Ripper. Robert Mann, an attendant at the Whitechapel mortuary, is also sometimes cited as a Jack the Ripper suspect. In the 1996 book Jack the Ripper, Light-Hearted Friend, it is suggested that the author Lewis Carroll was responsible for the Ripper murders. This theory is, you won't be surprised to hear, not taken very seriously. In 1992, a man named Michael Barrett claimed to have discovered the diary of Jack the Ripper in Liverpool. The diary revealed that the Ripper was James Maybrick - a person believed to have been poisoned by his wife. The diary naturally turned out to be a hoax.

Why Are There Less Serial Killers Today Than There Used To Be?

Serial killers today are at a low level compared to the 1970s, 80s, and even 90s. There are a number of factors for why this is the case. The fact that most nations have extensive CCTV camera systems in cities and towns now is one obvious reason why it's harder to be a serial killer today. If someone like Richard Ramirez or Ted Bundy was prowling suspiciously round some neighbourhood today they'd be picked up on multiple cameras very quickly. It would be very difficult today, for example, to break into an apartment building without being captured on camera. Home security systems and alarms are also better than they used to be. Most homes also have outdoor security lighting today.

Another important change from the serial killer festooned seventies and eighties is that many sex workers today operate online rather than walk the streets. They are able to 'vet' the people they meet more than was possible in the past. Now, this doesn't make them 100% safe but sex workers (so often the victims of famous serial killers) are a lot safer today than they used to be. Another theory for why there aren't as many serial killers is that the police have more technology at their disposal now and are simply better at catching murderers than they used to be. Forensics and DNA profiling is much more advanced today than it was in the 1970s.

If some of the more infamous serial killers from yesteryear were operating today they would almost certainly be captured a lot more quickly. Gary Ridgway first became a suspect in the Green River murders in 1982 but, unfortunately, nothing came of this. The police had insufficient evidence against him at the time. The fact that Gary Ridgway was the Green River Killer was only deduced in 2001 when his DNA (from a sample taken by the police in the 1980s) was matched to DNA found at one of the Green River Killer crime scenes. The police today can convict someone from a single strand of hair found at a crime scene. This sort of forensic technology means that serial killers today have no margin of error at all anymore.

One obvious theory as to why serial killer murders are not as common as they used to be is that modern society is less risk adverse than it was in the 1970s and 1980s. People and (especially) teenagers and children are more clued up about danger. Society, for better or worse, is less innocent than it used to be. Children and young people also go out less than they used. In the 1960s and 1970s it was common for teenagers and children to go out and roam free for hours. Nowadays, this doesn't happen so much. Children and young people tend to stay home more (where they have social media and ample entertainment technology). In the 1970s it was also fairly common for young women to hitchhike alone and take a lift from men they didn't know. This wouldn't happen so much today.

People of all ages also have mobile phones too so are always in contact and easy to trace. Even cars have a GPS now. All these things make it a lot more difficult to be a serial killer than it used to be. There are less vulnerable or transient potential victims around and murdering someone is a difficult thing to get away with in the technological world of today. One theory for the reduction in American serial killers in recent years is that the parole system has changed and there are longer sentences. There is less chance now of a dangerous individual being released.

Tragically, there are many cases of famous serial killers who were released from prison for sexual and violent crimes only to kill upon release. This wouldn't happen today. The authorities nowadays are much more stringent in criminal case studies and identifying who might be a risk to the public. Modern societies are much better at cataloguing those who are dangerous or have committed serious crimes. Edward Kemper killed his grandparents in 1964 when he was only fifteen years old. He was declared paranoid schizophrenic and sent to the

Atascadero State Hospital. Kemper was released from the Atascadero State Hospital when he was 21.

One of the reasons for Kemper's release was that the staff liked him. They even allowed Kemper to became an unofficial part of the staff and test new patients with them. They believed Kemper was cured and no danger to anyone. This would obviously prove to be a tragic mistake. It is highly doubtful that Kemper would be released today like this. Arthur Shawcross sexually abused and murdered a ten year-old boy in 1972 that he had taken fishing. This is believed to have been his first murder. Shawcross then murdered an eight year-old girl. He ended up in prison but they released him 1987. This was another tragic case of someone who should have been locked up forever being allowed to roam the streets again. Shawcross would never get out of prison today with two disturbing child murders to his name.

In the past it was sometimes common for those with criminal convictions for sexual crimes or violence to be able to hide their past history. In the late 1960s for example, John Wayne Gacy sexually assaulted a fifteen year-old boy named Donald Vorhees. Gacy was sentenced to ten years in prison for underage sexual assault but he was such a model prisoner he was out on parole after a couple of years. The authorities, sadly, seemed to somewhat lose track of Gacy after his release. He was able to go back into the community without it being public knowledge that he was a convicted sex offender. Gacy, famously, even dressed up as a clown to entertain the local children in his community.

Ian Huntley, the monster who killed the ten year-old girls Holly Wells and Jessica Chapman in 2003 in the English village of Soham, had once raped a teenager and been accused of indecent assault of a number of underage girls but Humberside Police had destroyed their files on him and not passed on any warnings about him to other police forces. These sorts of things would not happen today. Police forces have computer records and more contact with one another.

Gacy and Ian Huntley would be on sex offender registers today and the communities where they lived would know of their past crimes. Ian Huntley had even, despite his past, managed to get a job as a school janitor! That would definitely not happen today. If one were to apply for a job at a school today you would be vetted very thoroughly to make sure you posed no danger to children.

The gay community in London were never happy with the way the Dennis Nilsen case was reported in the British tabloids. The tabloids often gave one the impression that the gay community was rife with dangerous murderous predatory men preying on teenagers. Dennis Nilsen was obviously a tragic aberration though and no more representative of gay people than someone like Peter Sutcliffe was of heterosexual people. Because of the homophobia inherent in society and institutions at the time, the gay men who made up Nilsen's victims were like some forgotten section of society. This is something that (you'd hope and expect) wouldn't happen today.

'Why wasn't Nilsen caught earlier?' wrote Crime Investigation. 'Maybe it has to do with the victims he preyed upon and the police's attitude towards them. For years, Nilsen targeted the vulnerable: young men and boys (some as young as 14) who were part of groups that police have historically been accused of ignoring: most were gay, many were homeless and runaways and some were involved in sex work. When allegations against Nilsen surfaced, they were seemingly disregarded and dismissed by police, who wrote them off as 'gay crimes'. Can police homophobia account for the reason Nilsen wasn't caught sooner? It seems so.'

One other factor why there are less serial killers today is an improvement in living conditions and social services. This is not to say things are perfect (we still have poverty and inequality in modern societies) but the squalor and poverty some serial killers endured as children doesn't exist to day on the same level. This also means there are less victims available for serial killers (who tend to prey on the poor and disconnected member of society).

There are also more social interventions today that might have saved some serial killers of the past by taking them out of society and treating them before they became killers. We'd like to think that mental health and social care is something that has come on leaps and bounds in recent years. Maybe, just maybe, someone like a Jeffrey Dahmer, if he was a teenager today, might have been diagnosed and looked after before he began to spiral out of control.

Why Do Women Write To And Marry Incarcerated Serial Killers?

Ted Bundy was said to receive 200 letters a day from female 'groupies' while he was awaiting his last trials. Believe it or not, Bundy was even rumoured to have started a relationship with one of his lawyers. As unbelievable as it sounds, even the goofy looking Arthur Shawcross seemed to attract female fans in prison. The term for this strange phenomenon is hybristophilia. Hybristophilia is sometimes referred to as Bonnie and Clyde syndrome. 'Hybristophiliacs,' wrote Owlcation, 'are people who are sexually aroused and attracted to people who have committed cruel, gruesome crimes such as murder and rape. It occurs more often in women than in men. There are two categories of hybristophiliacs: The first is Passive Hybristophilia. Every year, notorious criminals receive romantic and sexual fan mail from admirers. These letter-writing groupies (known as SKGs -- serial killer groupies) have no desire in taking part of criminal activity, yet are attracted to men behind bars.

'These women are usually delusional and will try to find excuses for what the criminal did. They will develop relationships with a criminal and feel that they are special -- that even though their lover may have killed numerous people, he would never harm her. They usually feel that they can change their lover and have rescue fantasies. Passive hybristophiliacs tend to put themselves in positions to be seduced, manipulated, and lied to by the people they fall for. Aggressive hybristophiliacs are complete opposites. They are willing to help out their lovers with their criminal agenda by luring victims, hiding bodies, covering crimes, or even committing crimes. They are attracted to their lover's because of their violent actions and want to receive love, yet are unable to understand that their lover's are psychopaths who are manipulating them. Both passive and aggressive hybristophiliacs tend to end up in abusive or unhealthy relationships.'

Richard Ramirez was said to get plenty of fan mail in prison from women when he was arrested. When he was in prison, Ramirez married magazine editor Doreen Lioy. Lioy had been sending him dozens of letters. Doreen Lioy described Ramirez (who, lest we forget, once plucked out a victim's eyes and put them in a jewelry case for the police to find) as funny and charming. If that's not hybristophilia then nothing is. "I think he's a really great person. He's my best friend; he's my buddy," said Lioy. "I can't help the way the world looks at him. They don't know him the way I do. [People call me crazy] or stupid or lying, and I'm none of those things. I just believe in him completely. In my opinion, there was far more evidence to convict O.J. Simpson, and we all know how that turned out."

Ramirez died of secondary to B-cell lymphoma in 2013 at the age of 53. Doreen Lioy didn't seem to turn up to claim the body of Ramirez when he died in prison. Maybe she was in love with some other evil incarcerated serial killer by this time. In 2009 it had been proven beyond doubt by DNA technology that Richard Ramirez killed a nine year old girl named Mei Leung in 1984. Even the deluded and gullible Doreen Lioy must have felt very stupid and very appalled and disgusted by this scientific cold case revelation. Lioy was not the only person to find Ramirez attractive. Cynthia Haden, one of the jurors at his trial, fell in love with Ramirez and defended him in interviews.

Carol Ann Boone moved to Florida to support Ted Bundy when he was put on trial and served as a character witness for him. She accepted his marriage proposal and had a child with him. "Let me put it this way, I don't think that Ted belongs in jail," said Boone during the trials. "The things in Florida don't concern me any more than the things out west do. I don't think they have reason to charge Ted Bundy with murder in either Leon County or Columbia County." Boone was so devoted to Bundy she smuggled drugs into prison for him. There are even stories that she tried to help him escape. Carol Ann Boone always steadfastly insisted Bundy was innocent. However, Bundy later confessed to being a serial killer when he was on death row. He became confessional in an attempt to buy time and stall the electric chair. Carol Ann Boone, like Doreen Lioy, was exposed as a foolish and gullible woman.

"I can't tell you how often I see this (hybristophilia) happen," said Louis Schlesinger, PhD, professor of forensic psychology at the John Jay College Of Criminal Justice. "In nearly every penitentiary across the country you'll find female employees, like lawyers, therapists, and guards, getting involved with inmates." Jeffrey Ian Ross, PhD, criminologist and professor at the University of Baltimore, said of hybristophilia - "Basically, it's a sexual attraction to someone who's committed some sort of outrageous and extraordinary crime. Most of these women only see these men for occasional visits in their prison, during which, the man is on his best behaviour. If he's not, she may never come back again. They also don't have to deal with any of the disappointments that can come up in day-to-day in relationships." In a warped way then, you might describe an incarcerated serial killer as the perfect boyfriend!

Henry Lee Lucas, Arthur Shawcross, and Randall Woodfield are among the killers who got married in prison. Even Jeffrey Dahmer is said to have got fan mail. After his death, Dennis Nilsen's spectacles were given to a woman named Andrea Kubinova in the Czech Republic. Kubinova was Nilsen's pen pal and visited him in prison. "He came across as a nice person," she said. "I know it's odd in the context, but yeah he was." You might suggest that Eva Braun, Hitler's mistress and (briefly) wife, suffered from a form of hybristophilia. Afton Burton (aka Star) is the young woman who started contacting Charles Manson in prison and later became engaged to him. She was only 17 when she first contacted him. Burton described Manson as her idol and said she wanted to marry him. He kicked the bucket though before this could happen.

We see evidence of hybristophilia in some 'killer couples'. Myra Hindley was clearly in thrall to Ian Brady. Gerald and

Charlene Gallego became known as the Love Slave Killers in Sacramento, California. This was an unlikely duo. Gerald Gallego was a known criminal who once molested a child but Charlene Gallego was from a good family and intelligent. Nonetheless, they married and he exerted great control over her. Gerald Gallego's fantasy to was have 'love slaves' and Charlene facilitated this by helping him to lure victims to their van.

In 1978 Gerald Gallego raped and murdered two teenage girls that Charlene had found. He would kill five more people in 1980 - including one man. Gerald and Charlene Gallego were thankfully captured in 1980. Charlene agreed to testify against Charlene Gallego as part of a plea bargain that would reduce her sentence. He was sentenced to death but died of natural causes in prison in 2002. Charlene Gallego was released in 1997. She said she had tried to save the victims and did not participate in the murders. Many believe though that she was released far too early.

It seems that hybristophilia clouds any sense of logic or taste. Women (and sometimes men) are fascinated by serial killers and even become overwhelmed by the desire to meet them and look after them. They rationalise this conduct by refusing to believe the killer is guilty or simply tell themselves they are doing a kind deed to someone who is lonely and an outcast in society. No matter how awful the killer is, you can guarantee that killer has received fan mail and that there are probably women out there who would be perfectly willing to meet them and, in some cases, even marry them. Afton Burton and Doreen Lioy are far from unique. It seems that, for as long as serial killers exist, there will always be people trying to contact them from the outside world.

What Strange Serial Killer Memorabilia Can You Buy?

There is a lot of weird serial killer 'memorabilia' floating around. Murderabilia products is the general term for these items. Some of this is available to buy and some of it has only been put on display in museums (of the macabre). EBay banned the sale of serial killer artefacts on their sites in the end because they thought it was rather tasteless. True crime 'collectibles' websites though have all manner of stuff you can buy. For example, fancy owning a polaroid photograph of Arthur Shawcross for $275? No, me neither. A true crime collectible site put up for sale an Ambrosia chocolate factory paycheck made out to Jeffrey Dahmer. Dahmer's signature is on the back. The price you'd have to pay to own this paycheck? $15,000!

John Wayne Gacy is said to have done 2,000 paintings while he was on death row. The Tatou Art Gallery in Beverly Hills tried to sell some of John Wayne Gacy's paintings. They were described as art brut. He liked to paint Elvis, Jesus, skulls, and Disney characters. Gacy naturally did a few self-portraits too - complete with clown costume. Legend has it that Johnny Depp owns one of Gacy's paintings. Two businessmen eventually purchased many of John Wayne Gacy's prison paintings in the end and had them destroyed in a mass bonfire where people (including relatives of Gacy's victims) gathered and cheered. Paintings by Gacy still lurk around though and can go for high prices.

When it comes to serial killer art, John Wayne Gacy had a rival in the form of Donald Gaskins. You can buy a childish clown illustration that Gaskins did in prison for $350. John Wayne Gacy was an atrocious painter and illustrator and Gaskins was even worse. William Bonin is another dead serial killer who continues to inflict prison art on the public through crime collectibles websites. His signed painting Visions Of The Mind will set you back $10,000. Art by Herbert Mullin can fetch $400.

Ed Gein drove a 1949 Ford sedan. After Gein's arrest, an enterprising man purchased the car and charged the public 25 cents to have their picture taken with the vehicle. It is not known what happened to Ed Gein's car after it was confiscated from the man who was charging people to have their photograph taken with it. It was most likely junked. Artifacts that have made their way into museums and displays include, for some reason or other, the work boots of Fred West. Ted Bundy's Beetle car ended up in a museum. Karl Denke's gruesome workshop and knives became a macabre exhibit at Ziebice's Museum of Household Goods. John Haigh's gloves and apron (which he used to protect himself from burns from the acid bath) are displayed at New Scotland Yard's infamous Black Museum. The museum has also displayed Dennis Nilsen's stove.

True crime collectible sites used to sell dirt alleged to be from Ed Gein's farm. The obvious problem with this is that they probably just dug it up from their back garden! Who wants to own dirt from Ed Gein's farm anyway? Equally dubious is the ability to buy water taken from Herbert Baumeister's Fox Hollow Farm (where numerous bodies were dug up). A sample of water from Baumeister's farm will cost you $50. You can buy an ashtray that belonged to Richard Speck for $250 on a crime website. A polaroid of Richard Ramirez and Doreen Lioy together will set you back $350 on crime websites. Yeah, I think I'd pass on that one.

Some of the True Crime collectible sites sell a transcript of Jeffrey Dahmer's police confession. However, you can download this in PDF form for free if you look around. A signed self-portrait by Richard Ramirez (from when he was in prison obviously) can sell for around $3,500. The autograph of Albert Fish sold for $30,000 in 2010 on a crime website. John Wayne Gacy had two hand made clown suits which were both seized by the authorities when he was arrested. One of those suits was later sold by someone for $25,000 and then somehow ended up in the National Crime Museum. You can buy a Christmas card lovingingly handmade by John Wayne Gacy when he was in prison for $895.

Believe it or not, Peter Kürten's head was once displayed at Ripley's Believe It or Not in Wisconsin Dells. The blurb went like this - 'Beheaded murderer Peter Kurten had his head bisected and mummified in attempt by scientists to understand the workings of his mind. Tried for 68 ghoulish crimes, including 9 murders, Peter Kurten was sentenced to be beheaded in Germany in 1931. So demented was Kurten's behaviour, criminologists believed his brain had to be physically different from the norm in order for him to have concocted his grisly crimes. Therefore, his head was bisected to study his brain and the skull's internal cavities.'

A shirt worn by Richard Ramirez in prison can go for $9,000. Letters signed by Arthur Shawcross can fetch $50. The drain cover from Robert Berdella's basement is on sale for $2,000. Letters written by Ted Bundy can fetch up to $3,000. A signed prison photo of Rodney Alcala can set you back $600. Dennis Nilsen stuff on collectibles sites is quite rare although you can buy a letter he wrote for $200. A website called TeePublic.Com sells Dennis Nilsen 'retro serial killer' t-shirts and tops. A company called Kulturmeister produced some serial killer playing cards or Top Trumps. Nilsen features and has a 'maniac rating' of three stars. He tends to be dubbed The Company Killer in such things.

You can buy a copy of Ann Rule's The Stranger Beside Me signed by Ted Bundy. This item is valued at about $10,000. For $15 you can buy a photograph of Aileen Wuornos posing with a friend before her execution. A shirt worn by Peter Sutcliffe in prison can go for about $1,000 on collectibles websites. You used to be able to buy the 'Jeffrey Dahmer victim doll', which was 'fully dismemberable' and '100% cannibal approved.' This toy would have set you back $295. There has been a serial killer board game - which naturally created some controversy. The Crime Through Time museum in Gloucestershire is home to a shovel that belonged to Fred West.

You can buy a car licence plate that belonged to John Wayne Gacy on crime websites. A Valentines Day card from Jeffrey Dahmer can go for $5000. A brick from Ed Gein's local store wil cost you $75. An empty candy wrapper that Charles Manson used will go for $750. Who wants an empty candy wrapper? A football shirt worn by OJ Simpson will cost you $500. You can buy an Albert Fish action figure (this charming item has Fish brandishing a meat cleaver behind his back). You can buy a Gary Ridgway bobblehead. You can buy John Wayne Gacy's business card. You can buy a strand of Lawrence Bittaker's hair. You can buy a letter with the fingerprints of Tommy Lee Sells. You can even buy a pair of panties once owned by Aileen Wuornos.

When it comes to true crime memorabilia, you can buy literally anything. There is naturally a debate about the morality of this sort of business. Relatives of victims have raised a lot of concern. It would obviously be distressing to see some killer who had murdered one of your relatives turned into a bobblehead toy or trading card or grinning in some prison photograph. However, those who sell these items feel it is relatively harmless and liken it to those who have an interest in the occult or horror. People are naturally interested in dark things.

Which Serial Killers Appeared On Television Before We Knew They Were Serial Killers?

A number of serial killers appeared on television before we knew they were serial killers. The most famous of these TV appearances is probably that of Rodney Alcala. Alcala is retrospectively chilling because of his relative success in society. He went to college, appeared on television, worked as a photographer, and got employment in a summer camp. He was hiding in plain sight all the time. Alcala might have killed over a hundred people for all we know. Most of his victims will probably never be identified. In 1978, Alcala famously appeared as a contestant on the TV show The Dating Game. Alcala was introduced by the host as a successful photographer who enjoys skydiving. He was competing with two other male bachelors to win a date with the female contestant (through answers they gave to her questions from behind a screen). Alcala was chosen but the woman found him so creepy when the screen was removed that she refused to go on the date.

Alcala had long hair and was sort of good looking but there was definitely something of the night about him. He gave everyone the creeps. One of the male contestants on The Dating Game episode with Rodney Alcala said that Alcala had made his skin crawl that night. He described Alcala as an obnoxious creep. When he defended himself in court at his third trial, Alcala played a clip from his appearance on The Dating Game as part of his defence. What he hoped to achieve by this is anyone's guess. Perhaps the creepiest part of his appearance on The Dating Game came when Alcala was asked if he was a day person or a night person. Alcala replied that he was a night person and said all the best things happen at night. Given that he was in reality a serial killer this answer is all the more chilling.

John William Cooper was a killer in Britain who committed

two double murders in the 1980s. He was also responsible for a string of assaults and rape. In 1989, a month before he killed again, he appeared as a contestant on the popular darts themed TV game show Bullseye. Bullseye was a popular Sunday afternoon prime time quiz where people played darts to win prizes and money. Millions of people watched this show. Although he served time in prison for robbery, it was only in 2009 (thanks to advances in forensic science) that John William Cooper was arrested for the murders. He was convicted and given a life sentence in 2011. Cooper killed siblings Richard and Helen Thomas Peter and Gwenda Dixon. The murders were known in the media as the Pembrokeshire Murders or the Coastal Murders. The motive for murder was robbery.

John William Cooper was a sadistic and evil man. He used a shotgun in his murders and believed to have had over 30 convictions for sexual assault and robbery. He raped underage girls. Cooper was a farm labourer who won a considerable sum of money in a Spot the Ball competition (Spot the ball is a traditional newspaper promotion where the player has to guess the position of a ball which has been removed from a photograph of a ball sport) but he frittered the money away because of gambling and alcohol addictions. At some point this violent man became desperate enough to turn to crime and murder. Cooper seems placid and friendly on Bullseye. At the start he says he is a fan of scuba diving. It just goes to how you that serial killers come in all guises and are not always easy to spot.

Harold Shipman (the GP who killed hundreds of his own patients) appeared on the British documentary television show World in Action in 1982 talking about new treatments for the mentally ill. You'd never guess in a million years that Shipman was a serial killer from watching his appearance in this documentary. 'HAROLD Shipman made an appearance on the television programme World in Action in 1982, talking about caring for patients in the community,' wrote the Manchester Evening News when the footage was unearthed. 'Interviewed at his desk at Donneybrook House, a group practice in Hyde, Shipman talks enthusiastically about a new type of treatment for the mentally ill. The footage was rediscovered nearly 20 years later and aired in 2000, months after he had been convicted for the murder of 15 patients at Preston Crown Court.

'Shipman - aged 37 at the time - said: "If you can stay in the community and receive your treatment in the community and if you have your family around you and your usual friends, then this all adds to the speed of the recovery from the illness." The medic also adds: "It means that someone can go and be seen at Brindle House directly from our surgery and they can walk up the road and be seen within half an hour. In the past, if a patient had got a mental illness that required admission to hospital then the patient was formally admitted, undressed and placed into a bed and was treated though they had a physical illness. A consultant would often come around in a white coat and there was an invisible barrier between the patient and the doctor."'

Stephen Port is a rapist and killer who murdered four men in London from 2014 to 2015. He would drug them with GBH (gamma-Hydroxybutyric acid - known as a 'date rape' drug). Three of the victims were disposed of in a graveyard by Port. He was given life in prison. Stephen Port, who worked as a chef in a bus depot, once appeared on television as a kitchen assistant in the popular BBC show Masterchef. The BBC have now edited him out of that episode. Port was a very dangerous and ruthless man. He was overwhelmed by his fantasy of having sex with victims who were inert or helpless (this is, as we have noted, a common theme in serial killers). Port even faked suicide notes for some of his victims and this made the police slow in connecting the deaths. Port met his victims through online dating apps and this case led to some understandable concern over their safety.

Dennis Rader appeared on a local TV news station in 1991 in an item that seem to be about stray dogs. Rader was seen in his duties as a Compliance Officer talking about animal attacks. He had a uniform and gun and sounded just like any other jobsworth petty official. You might even say that Dennis Rader seemed boring and dull in real lie. If you watched this news clip you might think this man was rather humourless and slightly stern but you'd never in a million years think he was a serial killer. That was the reason why Rader got away with his crimes for so long. He was an Average Joe. A dull bald family man with a mustache and children. No one knew that he had the most depraved and sadistic private life imaginable. It's strange to watch the clip of Rader on this news channel now with the knowledge that he murdered families and hung an eleven year-old girl from a basement pipe.

Ian Huntley is a notorious and much despised true crime figure in Britain for killing the ten year-old girls Holly Wells and Jessica Chapman in the village of Soham in Cambridgeshire in 2003. Huntley was the 28 year-old caretaker at Soham Village College - the school that Holly and Jessica attended. Huntley told the police he was the last person to speak to the girls before they went missing because they had walked past his house on their way to a shop to buy some sweets. Huntley was shrewd. He volunteered this information because he thought it would make him less suspicious. In reality he had murdered the girls (in circumstances which remain vague because he never confessed or discussed the murders).

Huntley lingered on at the scene of the crime in the middle of police investigations and escalating media scrutiny. In this one might argue that he had little choice. To flee would be to draw suspicion. He even ended up as a fairly regular person for television news crews to interview. Huntley was meek and articulate when he spoke to the media. He was perfectly calm and even conveyed a projection of simulated empathy. There was a very small window in time where Ian Huntley might possibly have felt as if he was in control of events in Soham. He might even have felt he stood a slim chance of getting away with his crimes

It was often said of Ian Huntley that he seemed to enjoy the attention when he lingered on in Soham after murdering Holly Wells and Jessica Chapman. Huntley gave television interviews for the nightly news and was prominent at community meetings and candlelight vigils. He seemed to be taking satisfaction in the (ultimately mistaken) belief that he had pulled the wool over everyone's eyes. When the two girls in Soham went missing and Ian Huntley was interviewed on television, no one watching at home had a sudden sixth sense that he was the person responsible. Huntley was not overtly and obviously suspicious. Huntley had managed to move the bodies of Holly and Jessica after he had killed them to a quiet country footpath near RAF Lakenheath. He had then tried to burn the bodies to destroy the evidence. Ironically, it was Huntley's television interviews that gave him away.

During one television news interview, Ian Huntley was interviewed outside of his house with his car next to him. Police detectives who watched this interview noticed that Huntley had new tyres on his car. The tyres were very clean and sparkling. They were clearly brand new. The area around Soham was quite rural and featured a lot of footpaths and roads that had very distinctive pebbles and sand. Huntley was trying to hide the fact that he'd driven up these backroads (with the bodies of Holly and Jessica). Thankfully, the net closed around this awful man quite quickly in the end and he was taken into custody. Huntley was charged with murder and given two life sentences. The clips of Huntley on the news now are fascinating in retrospect. It's amazing, given the circumstances, how calm and collected he was.

Two Hundred Strange But True Serial Killer Facts

(1) Dennis Nilsen would sometimes lose track of where he had left body parts and was surprised once to open a cupboard door and find a pair of severed legs inside.

(2) Ever wonder why Ted Bundy absolutely adored the Volkswagen Beetle? He even stole one of these cars when he escaped from prison. Bundy liked this car because you could take out the passenger seat (and thus make it easier to get a body or person into the car and put it in the back seat).

(3) In his duties as director of Chicago's Polish Constitution Day Parade, John Wayne Gacy was personally introduced to the First Lady of the United States Rosalynn Carter in 1978. She obviously had no idea she was meeting one of the worst serial killers in American history.

(4) When he was captured, Richard Chase said he killed to protect himself from aliens and that the Nazis had framed him.

(5) When he was briefly a security guard, Dennis Nilsen said he once tried to have sex with a stuffed gorilla in the Natural History Museum.

(6) Marion Albert Pruett, who killed at least five people in 1981, was in the witness protection program when he first killed. He had given evidence about a prison slaying - so was under protection.

(7) About 3% of executions in the United States have gone wrong in some way. Mishaps have included people catching fire in the electric chair and decapitations during hanging.

(8) Ray and Faye Copeland are - at 76 and 69 - the oldest

couple to be sentenced to death in the United States. They conspired to murder five farm workers on their farm in Mooresville, Missouri between 1986 and 1989. Ray Copeland used the farm workers (who were drifters looking for work) to buy cattle with dodgy cheques and then shot the workers so that nothing could be traced back to him. Fay was judged to be in on their murderous scheme. Neither Ray or Faye Copeland were executed in the end. Ray Copeland died in prison in 1993 and Faye Copeland, who had her sentence commuted to life in prison for manslaughter, died in 2002. Faye Copeland died in a nursing home after Governor Bob Holden agreed to a request for a medical parole.

(9) When Ed Kemper telephoned the police to confess to murder, they hung up on him at first because they thought he was drunk or goofing around. Kemper was friends with a lot of the local cops because they drank at the same bars.

(10) On his last day at work as a civil servant, Dennis Nilsen wore a scarf that had belonged to his last victim Stephen Sinclair. Nilsen told office colleagues that he if he wasn't at work the next day it would be because he was either dead or in prison. They all thought he was joking and laughed.

(11) Jeffrey Dahmer's name has thirteen letters. His murder spree lasted for thirteen years. Guess what his apartment number was? That's right. Number 13.

(12) Ted Bundy was an expert shoplifter. Most of the stuff he owned was usually stolen.

(13) Estate agents who try to sell the two flats where Dennis Nilsen used to live are obliged to warn prospective buyers about the dark history of the properties. It doesn't seem to have put people off though.

(14) The youngest serial killer is usually cited as Amardeep Sada. Amardeep Sada killed three people in India when he was eight years-old. The victims were all children and included

Sada's sister.

(15) When he first tried to put a victim's body under the floorboards, Dennis Nilsen found it impossible because rigor mortis had set in. He had to manipulate the limbs to make the body more flexible.

(16) Of her victim blood cakes, Leonarda Cianciulli said - "I threw the pieces into a pot, added seven kilos of caustic soda, which I had bought to make soap, and stirred the mixture until the pieces dissolved in a thick, dark mush that I poured into several buckets and emptied in a nearby septic tank. As for the blood in the basin, I waited until it had coagulated, dried it in the oven, ground it and mixed it with flour, sugar, chocolate, milk and eggs, as well as a bit of margarine, kneading all the ingredients together. I made lots of crunchy tea cakes and served them to the ladies who came to visit, though Giuseppe and I also ate them."

(17) Dennis Nilsen was a union representative for the civil service. Nilsen was apparently a very pedantic and dogged union rep.

(18) Believe it or not, the guillotine was used in France to execute the worst criminals until 1977.

(19) In Inside Time (a newspaper for prisoners and detainees), someone who once spent time in prison with Dennis Nilsen said Nilsen would constantly cheat when they played Scrabble.

(20) Ted Bundy's aunt once awoke to find Bundy, still a child at the time, placing knives around her sleeping form.

(21) Dennis Nilsen liked to make mulled wine for his work colleagues at Christmas.

(22) Rodney Alcala killed Ellen Jane Hover - who was the goddaughter of Dean Martin and Sammy Davis Jr.

(23) When he had bonfires at Melrose Avenue, Dennis Nilsen always had to tell curious children to keep back in case they might see any human remains or bones.

(24) Peter Sutcliffe was initially arrested for driving a vehicle with a false number plate. It was only when they had him in custody for this that the police noticed he shared a lot of similarities with the suspect profile for The Yorkshire Ripper.

(25) Danny Rolling was very fond of taking acid 'trips'- something he did at least a hundred times.

(26) Ed Kemper has narrated audio books for the blind while in prison. He is said to have completed several hundred recordings.

(27) Dennis Nilsen would sometimes cook his dinner in another pan at the same time that he was boiling a head on the other hob ring.

(28) Ted Bundy once saved a toddler from drowning. This happened at Green Lake in Seattle in 1970. Bundy noticed the child struggling in the water and dived in to save him.

(29) The capture of serial killer Luis Garavito was a lucky fluke. Garavito had been arrested for attempted rape but the officers who had him in custody were not aware he was a suspect in any murders. Thankfully, Garavito cracked and confessed all.

(30) When he was a teenage army recruit, Dennis Nilsen went on camping trips to the New Forest and Stonehenge.

(31) Ed Gein was found to have a belt made from female human nipples.

(32) When the police searched the home of the 'foot fetish' serial killer Jerry Brudos they found that he not only had photographs of his dead victims but that he had also taken

photographs of their severed feet.

(33) Most serial killers are surprisingly ordinary and dull in person. This would explain why so many of them seem to have unsuspecting wives and families.

(34) In 1983, The Guardian reported that Dennis Nilsen had once left a bag of human intestines at a bus stop.

(35) In 2018, a Japanese eatery called Ningu served recreations of the last meal requests of famous serial killers.

(36) Dennis Rader's letters to the police were so riddled with grammatical errors and spelling mistakes that the police thought the BTK killer must be doing this on purpose. It turned out he wasn't though. Rader just wasn't very good at spelling and writing.

(37) After one of his home invasion murders, Richard Ramirez would sometimes eat everything in the fridge and then hang around the house for a while to enjoy his gruesome handiwork.

(38) Convicted killer Romell Broom was spared the death penalty in Ohio because when it was time for his execution they couldn't find a suitable vein to give him a lethal injection.

(39) Albert Fish liked to be hit with a spiked cane.

(40) One of the things that helped convict the Golden State Killer was the surviving victims all testifying that he had small genitalia.

(41) Dennis Rader studied criminal justice in college.

(42) When he was growing-up, Jeffrey Dahmer stole a mannequin from a store and kept it in his bedroom.

(43) When the actor Sean Penn (who was famously obstreperous and known to punch journalists) served some

time in L.A County jail in 1987, he discovered that Richard Ramirez was in the same prison. Ramirez had a fan letter passed to Penn.

(44) Dennis Nilsen said he would put underwear, socks, and a vest on the bodies of his dead victims when he brought them out to watch television with.

(45) The apple fritter was said to be a very popular choice at Robert Hansen's Alaska bakery.

(46) The police had to use an anthropologist to try and make sense of the bones and remains found in the wake of Dennis Nilsen's arrest.

(47) After someone is killed in the electric chair, they have to wait for the body to cool down before they perform an autopsy.

(48) When he acted as his own lawyer in court, Rodney Alcala tried to cross examine himself.

(49) When the police asked Dennis Nilsen how many bodies he had under the floorboards he replied - "I didn't do a stock check."

(50) Carroll Edward Cole was found to have an IQ of 152. This would place him at the top end of serial killers when it comes to intelligence.

(51) The police had to 're-assemble' Dennis Nilsen's last victim on a mortuary slab to identify him.

(52) There is a theory that H.H. Holmes could have been Jack the Ripper but the evidence is vague at best. The vast geographical distance between the two sets of murders alone makes it unlikely.

(53) In a story so bizarre it sounds completely made up, after his execution there was a battle for custody of Jeffrey

Dahmer's brain between the prison authorities and the Dahmer family.

(54) In the book House of Horrors by John Lisners, it is alleged that a former police colleague of Dennis Nilsen, on hearing later about the grisly story of murder unfolding at Cranley Gardens in the early 1980s, said - "If it's an ex-copper my money is on Dennis Nilsen."

(55) The last public execution held in the United States was in 1936. They used to get good crowds at public hangings.

(56) Joey "The Cannibal" Methney is a killer convicted of two murders. He might have killed thirteen people in all. Methney would put the blood of his victims in the burgers he sold at his food stall.

(57) When he was finally convicted for his many murders, Gary Ridgeway was moved to tears in court when the very religious father of one of his victims said that he forgave Ridgeway.

(58) Dennis Nilsen said that he would shave his victims as part of the process of 'caring' for their bodies.

(59) Former police detective Michael Arntfield believes that the number of serial killers at large in America at any one time is underestimated. He has stated that there is a 40% chance of getting away with murder - a fact which (if true) would indicate that a number of serial killers could fly under the radar so to speak.

(60) Ed Gein had nine vulvae in a shoe-box when the police searched his farmhouse.

(61) More than 1,000 pieces of flesh and bone were found by forensic teams and police officers at the two London flats Dennis Nilsen had lived in.

(62) Kendall Francois was a serial killer arrested in 1998 in Poughkeepsie. When the police searched his house they found that he had some of the skulls of his victims in a plastic kiddie pool in the attic.

(63) Dennis Nilsen said that he sometimes used to bathe in the same water that he had used to wash the bodies of his victims.

(64) Most serial killers are judged to be sane when they are captured and tested.

(65) In 2012, Matthew Milat, the great-nephew of the notorious backpacker killer Ivan Milet, was convicted of killing a man with an axe and filming it on his phone. "That's what the Milats do," Matthew Milat is alleged to have written of the murder.

(66) When the authorities demolished the house of Fred West at 25 Cromwell Street, they crushed every single brick and beam of wood so that ghoulish souvenir hunters wouldn't be able to take anything.

(67) Richard Chase was so insane he thought he would turn into powder and dust if he didn't drink blood on a regular basis.

(68) Ed Gein told the police that he never had sex with the bodies he dug up because they smelled too bad.

(69) Dennis Nilsen liked to write poetry and campaigned in prison to get his poetry published. In a strange quirk of fate, Nilsen had dealings with a probation officer in Wakefield Prison named Simon Armitage. Armitage later became the poet laureate (an honorary position appointed by the monarch). As you might expect, the poetry of Dennis Nilsen was pretty bizarre. One of his poems was all about condoms.

(70) A lethal injection will kill someone in less than five minutes. Three different drugs are used. Sodium thiopental

renders you unconscious, pancuronium bromide stops you breathing, and potassium chloride stops the heart.

(71) When he was a child, Ed Kemper would cut the heads off his sister's dolls and play a game where he pretended he was putting them in a gas chamber.

(72) Ed Gein's gravestone was stolen in 2000. It was eventually recovered and put in a museum.

(73) Joseph James DeAngelo called his urge to kill 'Jerry'. He described it as like having a persuasive demon on his shoulder.

(74) When he was a police constable, Dennis Nilsen said that he once found the body of a teenage girl in the morgue attractive and exciting because she looked like a little boy.

(75) The New York Mafia got involved in the search for the Son of Sam killer.

(76) Since 1976, twenty-two minors (people under eighteen) have been executed in the United States. In 2005, the Supreme Court brought the United States into compliance with the international norm and ruled that the Constitution protects people from being sentenced to death for crimes committed when they were under 18.

(77) Ed Gein would dance around his farm at night wearing his human skin suits and mask.

(78) In 1994, Dennis Nilsen telephoned the author Brian Masters (who had interviewed Nilsen and written a book about him) from prison to say he didn't want to talk to him anymore. Masters was at the Garrick Club in London. When he heard that Dennis Nilsen was on the phone Masters went into a panic for a second because he thought Nilsen might have escaped from prison!

(79) Danny Rollings took home the nipples of one of his

victims as a trophy.

(80) Robert Pickton was found to have a dildo on the barrel of his revolver as a silencer.

(81) A band called Macabre wote a song about Dennis Nilsen called You're Dying to Be with Me. It was on their 2003 album Murder Metal.

(82) When Ted Bundy was executed, a huge group of people gathered outside the prison to throw a party and let off fireworks. Bundy could hear them cheering and laughing as he went to the death chamber.

(83) Dennis Nilsen tried to instigate legal action at Whitemoor Prison because he was not allowed access to gay nude magazines.

(84) Joachim Kroll was made to go back to his crime scenes by the police so he could explain everything that happened. Kroll even had to re-enact his abductions and attacks with an actress.

(85) The only countries that have more executions than the United States are China, Iran, Saudi Arabia, Iraq, Pakistan, Egypt, and Somalia.

(86) When Myra Hindley died in 2002, over twenty undertakers refused to handle the cremation. She was still one of the most despised people in Britain.

(87) Jeffrey Dahmer once planned to kill a jogger who ran past his building each day. The jogger suddenly stopped running past though.

(88) Dennis Nilsen would sometimes take food into work for colleagues. This food was almost certainly cooked in the same pot that he used to boil the heads of his victims.

(89) Case studies have suggested that 4% of condemned death row prisoners in the United States are innocent and were wrongly convicted.

(90) China does not reveal any statistics on how many criminals are executed in the country each year. It is estimated though that China executes well over two thousand people a year. That would make China comfortably top of the list of number of executions carried out by nations who still have the death penalty. Perhaps this fact isn't that strange really. You don't tend to think of the Chinese government as a humane institution.

(91) Richard Ramirez surprised everyone when he was interviewed in prison on television because he seemed perfectly calm and sane. Ramirez was clearly on his best behaviour for this interview and remained polite and reasonable.

(92) More serial killers have been born in November than any other month.

(93) After his arrest, Dennis Nilsen's last flat was decorated and put back on the market at £60,000 (this was 1983). The tabloids dubbed the flat the 'house of horrors' and wondered who on earth would want to live there. A surprisingly large number of people viewed the flat merely so they could gawp at the place where all these grisly and awful things took place.

(94) When the police found Annie Chapman after her murder by Jack the Ripper, her bladder had been removed and taken. It is presumed that the killer had taken the bladder away as a grisly trophy.

(95) The serial killer Arthur Shawcross once saved the life of a prison officer during a riot.

(96) Ed Kemper killed a 15-year-old Korean hitchhiker named Aiko Koo in 1972. He cut off the head of the victim and buried

it in his mother's back yard facing the house.

(97) Richard Ramirez drew a pentagram on the wall in lipstick after one of his murders. The pentagram is often portrayed as a symbolic representation of Satanism. The true meaning of the symbol is to ward off evil.

(98) Around 25% of serial killers murder with a partner or accomplice as opposed to killing alone.

(99) A homeless man looking for food near the building where Anthony (The Camden Ripper) Hardy lived was rather surprised when he rummaged through some bins and found a pair of severed human legs.

(100) When he was in the police, Dennis Nilsen once took a young man back to the Section House (a dorm for unmarried police officers) and had sex with him. The next morning, the sergeant was very suspicious when he saw the young man with Nilsen. The quick thinking Nilsen told his sergeant that the young man had just popped in because he was selling him a fish tank.

(101) Joe Aloi, who worked as an investigator for the circuit public defenders office, said of Ted Bundy - "I spent approximately nine months straight in a cell with him, three to eight hours a day sometimes. Bundy was a truly evil person, an exceptionally sick individual and he was a master at playing games. Bundy was the purest classical form of sociopathic personality. His evil was so strong, I was with him on two occasions that I saw physical changes in him. I could smell him. I was seriously afraid of him, and I'm not the type to get afraid. One of the times was when Kimberly Leach was found. He got very weird and very dissociative. He became very irate. He gave off an odour of almost burning carpet. He was just sweating profusely, almost like a chemical scent. He told me about this before. He was aware of it. It was wild, just incredible. I'm not saying this to glamourise Bundy. He was just trash. Bundy told me a lot of things I didn't want to

repeat. I don't want to hurt (his victims') families."

(102) The knife wound on Nicole Brown Simpson's neck was so severe it had penetrated a depth of .75 inches into her cervical vertebrae, nearly decapitating her.

(103) Dennis Nilsen is far from the only serial killer to write an autobiography while in prison. Donald "Pee Wee" Gaskins, Ian Brady, Myra Hindley, and Danny Rollings, amongst others, also wrote autobiographies while in prison. Few of these books were ever published. The problem with the 'memoirs' of serial killers is that we don't know what is embellished or fictional. Serial killers are not always reliable narrators. These books are rightly suppressed anyway.

(104) Jeffrey Dahmer was a famed prankster when he was at high school and had a good sense of humour.

(105) Despite murdering his grandparents, Ed Kemper was released from the Atascadero State Hospital when he was 21. His probation officer explained the decision to release him in the following appraisal of Kemper written at the time - 'If I were to see this patient without having any history available or getting any history from him, I would think that we're dealing with a very well adjusted young man who had initiative, intelligence and who was free of any psychiatric illnesses. It is my opinion that he has made a very excellent response to the years of treatment and rehabilitation and I would see no psychiatric reason to consider him to be of any danger to himself or to any member of society... [and] since it may allow him more freedom as an adult to develop his potential, I would consider it reasonable to have a permanent expunction of his juvenile records.'

(106) Dennis Nilsen once said - "You know, you'd be surprised how heavy a human head is when you pick it up by the hair."

(107) When he first came under suspicion, John Wayne Gacy tried to put a restraining order on the cops who had him under

surveillance. If he noticed any detectives following him, Gacy would go and knock on their car window and invite them to have breakfast. It was basically a display of bluff and bluster to make it seem as if he was was not worried but the reality is that he WAS worried and knew his days were numbered.

(108) When he visited Madame Tussauds as an army recruit, Dennis Nilsen viewed the replica bath of 'acid bath murderer' John Haigh. This is all rather ironic because Dennis Nilsen's own bath would later end up in a macabre museum of the bizarre.

(109) Richard Chase believed that an unlocked door was a signal to go inside and do whatever he wanted to.

(110) Donald Henry Gaskins evaded the death penalty at his trial but then - in a quirk of fate - was THEN given the death penalty for killing death row inmate Rudolph Tyner in prison. Gaskins was killed by electric chair in 1991

(111) Timothy Evans, the lodger of John Christie, was hung for the murder of his wife and daughter when in fact it was Christie who had killed them. John Christie was eventually hung by the same hangman who executed Timothy Evans.

(112) Dennis Nilsen's trip outside at night to remove the evidence from the drain at Cranley Gardens was almost certainly doomed from the start. Nilsen, on a tentative first attempt to explore the drain at night, was spotted by one of the other residents and asked what he was doing. Nilsen said that he had come out for a pee but he didn't seem convincing.

(113) During the preparation for the Richard Ramirez trial, one of the jurors was shot dead. This created much publicity with speculation that Ramirez had somehow orchestrated the death from prison to influence the jury. There was of course no actual truth to this rumour.

(114) Before his first hitchhiker murder, Ed Kemper is said to

have picked up as many as 150 hitchhikers without harming them. Kemper estimated that he picked up 1,000 hitchhikers in all.

(115) Jack Unterweger was an Austrian serial killer. His was a story so strange you couldn't make it up. In 1976 he was convicted for murdering a sex worker and sent to prison.

Unterweger wrote an autobiography in prison where he talked about his awful childhood and how he was now reformed. He attracted supporters charmed by his book and in 1990 he was released - becoming something of a celebrity and appearing on talk shows. A film about him was soon planned and he became a journalist. The only problem was that he wasn't really reformed. He started killing again and in 1994 was convicted of nine murders. He hung himself in prison.

(116) Rose West, the infamous wife of the equally infamous Fred West, was a prostitute who worked from home at 25 Cromwell Street. Fred West installed a secret camera so that he could surreptitiously film her sessions with clients. He then tried to interest local video stores in this material as 'special' under the counter stuff. To the great surprise of absolutely no one, the video stores were not interested and declined to purchase these grubby and grim home sex films.

(117) Richard Ramirez (thankfully) didn't last very long when he was a porter at a Holiday Inn because he was caught stealing from the guests. You definitely wouldn't want to stay at a hotel where Richard Ramirez was one of the porters!

(118) Ed Gein asked for a slice of apple pie with cheese on top before he would speak to investigators. When Travis Bickle orders apple pie with cheese in the film Taxi Driver this is a reference to Ed Gein. Apple pie with cheese is something of an acquired taste (most people would rather have custard or ice cream) and dates back to England (where the apple pie was invented).

(119) The police already had another suspect in custody when they deduced that Steven Wright was The Suffolk Strangler. The suspect (who was of course innocent) was actually a man suggested to the police by the media pack in East Anglia. The media had noticed this man hanging around a lot and simply didn't like the look of him. This amateur detective work on the part of the media was very wide of the mark and the man was released. This was a classic example of why the media and general public should leave detective work to the real detectives!

(120) Psychiatrists have speculated that killers who work in the medical world develop a 'God complex' and 'get off' on the fact that they have the power of life and death over their patients.

(121) FBI Agent Bill Hagmaier interviewed Ted Bundy in prison. Hagmaier said that Bundy confessed to cutting off the heads of his victims with a hacksaw and said he once had three heads in his apartment.

(122) Jeffrey Dahmer had two hands and genitalia floating in his kettle when the police searched his apartment.

(123) Ed Gein often acted as a babysitter for some of his neighbours. Gein was a childlike man himself and so got on well with children. There were never any incidents of Gein abusing or mistreating children.

(124) In 2011, a 17 year-old in Florida named Tyler Hadley invited sixty people to a party at his house. He told his friends that his parents had gone away for the weekend. Once the party was in full swing, Hadley confessed what had really happened. He had killed his parents with a clawhammer and the bodies were still upstairs. Tyler Hadley was too young to be executed and so received a life sentence in prison for his unfathomable crimes.

(125) Dennis Nilsen is believed to have transcribed 184 books

into Braille while he was in prison.

(126) John E. Robinson has been dubbed the first ever Internet serial killer. Robinson's victims were women he had made contact with through online chatrooms.

(127) The Golden State Killer had a habit of helping himself to snacks from the fridge during his terrifying home invasions. This is something he had in common with Richard Ramirez.

(128) The letter by Ted Bundy's sister Linda (which was read out in court after he was put on trial for attempted abduction) went like this - 'I am Ted Bundy's sister Linda. I am 23 years old and know very well what is going on. I know my brother and how interested and concerned he always has been about people and he would never hurt anyone. I love my brother very much. I believe in him when he says that he did not [intend] to hurt that girl. My brother worked very hard to get somewhere in life. It was not easy, going to school and working to pay his way through school. My brother wants to be a good lawyer so that he can help people. He would never hurt anyone. My brother is not a kidnapper I'm sure. I know one time when he saved a little girl from drowning and another time when a man took a lady's purse and ran off and my brother caught him and got the lady's purse back. My brother is a good man. I cannot understand how you think that my brother could have kidnapped that girl. That it was no hard found evidence that proved beyond a shadow of a doubt that my brother did what you said he did. I know that he did not do it. Ted has always been very concerned about his family. I can remember one time when he was home I understand my sister [Sandra] was going out. My brother asked who she was going out with and where was she going because he was concerned. He has been concerned about me and my family because I live alone with my two children. Even though he was away from home and busy with work and school he always found time to call to see that everyone was alright. Ted has always been concerned about my brother, Glen as to what he was going to do when he was done with high school. I know that he has talked to my

parents about getting Glen to get a job or to go into college. He is now in the Navy. Ted has always been a very special person to our little brother, Richard. We all believe in our brother and believe him when he says that he did not kidnap a girl. We know he is not guilty because we know him better than anyone else does. I love my brother very much and believe in him. My brother has lots of friends and they all believe in him, too. Thank you for taking time to read my letter. I am sure you are a good man, too. Sincerely, Linda J. Bundy'

(129) After he washed the bodies of his victims, Dennis Nilsen would put talcum powder on them.

(130) Retired FBI agent John Bassett once speculated that Ted Bundy might have been responsible for the murder of a young woman who was killed in 1971 next to the Elizabeth Lund Home for Unwed Mothers in Vermont. The Elizabeth Lund Home for Unwed Mothers is where Ted Bundy was born. A man named Bundy was found to have been in town when the murder happened. That doesn't sound like a coincidence.

(131) The Japanese killer Tsutomu Miyazaki once cut off the hands of a victim and drank the blood from them.

(132) The Moors Murderer Ian Brady said that as a boy on his paper round he encountered the face of Death - who showed him the vision of children on a moor. Brady, in his own mind, saw the Moors Murders as a sacrificial offering to the 'Death' figure who had visited him as a child. Brady's childhood 'vision' is probably explained by the fact that he had a form of epilepsy which left him prone to hallucinations.

(133) Dennis Nilsen was very reluctant to consent to a plea of diminished responsibility. Despite his situation, his immense vanity made it difficult for him to accept that there was anything 'diminished' about his personality.

(134) Ed Kemper once apologised to a victim for touching her breast. He still killed her though.

(135) A few years before he died, Dennis Nilsen supposedly contributed to a horror novel by someone named Matthew Malekos. Matthew Malekos is an ex-psychiatric nurse who corresponded with Nilsen and had obviously tried to come up with some way to make money from this connection.

(136) The Son of Sam killer was said to target women with shoulder-length brunette hair. This had brunettes with shoulder-length hair in the Bronx all rushing to the hairdressers to radically alter their appearance.

(137) Paula Clennell, one of the victims of the Suffolk Strangler, was interviewed on the television news two weeks before she went missing. Paula, a prostitute, was asked why she was still on the street when there was a serial killer targeting sex workers in the area. She said she had no choice because she needed the money.

(138) The police found a collection of dolls in the home of Joachim Kroll. He said he used these dolls to try out techniques for abducting and restraining children.

(139) Stephen Shaun Griffiths became known as the Crossbow Cannibal. He killed three prostitutes in Bradford from 2008 to 2010. Griffiths was not really a cannibal although he was supposed to have fired a crossbow bolt at one victim. Griffiths pleaded guilty to all three murders. The remains of one victim have yet to be found. Griffiths would throw the bodies and remains in a river. Believe it or not, Stephen Shaun Griffiths was studying at Bradford University for a doctorate in criminology.

(140) John A. Cameron, a retired detective, wrote a book in which he claimed that Ed Edwards (a killer convicted of five murders) was not only the Zodiac killer but also the Black Dahlia killer. Cameron also claims that Edwards murdered JonBenet Ramsey and Jimmy Hoffa. You probably won't be surprised to hear that the book is not taken all that seriously.

Just about the only thing that Cameron didn't accuse Edwards of was smuggling Hitler out of his Berlin bunker to Argentina.

(141) In 2005, a Japanese schoolgirl was arrested for poisoning her mother with thallium. She had become obsessed with the story of Graham Young after watching The Young Poisoner's Handbook.

(142) Westley Allan Dodd was a child killer sentenced to death in 1990. Under Washington state law, Dodd was given the choice of hanging or lethal injection. He chose hanging as he had murdered one of his victims by this method and felt it would be fitting.

(143) Peter Sutcliffe was interviewed nine separate times by the police before he was actually arrested and revealed to be The Yorkshire Ripper.

(144) The most infamous crime of Albert Fish came when he pretended to be hiring farm workers and met the Budd family (whose father Edward was seeking employment). Fish persuaded them to let their ten year-old daughter Grace visit Fish to attend a birthday party for his niece but - of course - it was all a ruse and Grace turned up to find Fish alone. Fish later sent the Budd family a letter in which he claimed to have cooked and eaten Grace after he killed her. 'My dear Mrs Budd, In 1894 a friend of mine shipped as a deck hand on the steamer Tacoma, Capt John Davis. They sailed from San Francisco to Hong Kong China. On arriving there he and two others went ashore and got drunk. When they returned the boat was gone. At that time there was a famine in China. Meat of any kind was from $1 to 3 Dollars a pound. So great was the suffering among the very poor that all children under 12 were sold to the Butchers to be cut up and sold for food in order to keep others from starving.

'A boy or girl under 14 was not safe in the street. You could go in any shop and ask for steak – chops – or stew meat. Part of the naked body of a boy or girl would be brought out and just what you wanted cut from it. A boy or girls behind which is the sweetest part of the body and sold as veal cutlet brought the highest price. John staid there so long he acquired a taste for human flesh. On his return to N.Y. he stole two boys one 7 one 11. Took them to his home stripped them naked tied them in a closet then burned everything they had on. Several times every day and night he spanked them – tortured them – to make their meat good and tender. First he killed the 11 yr old boy, because he had the fattest ass and of course the most meat on it. Every part of his body was cooked and eaten except Head – bones and guts. He was roasted in the oven, (all of his ass) boiled, broiled, fried, stewed.

'The little boy was next, went the same way. At that time I was living at 409 E 100 St, rear – right side. He told me so often how good human flesh was I made up my mind to taste it. On Sunday June the 3 – 1928 I called on you at 406 W 15 St. Brought you pot cheese – strawberries. We had lunch. Grace sat in my lap and kissed me. I made up my mind to eat her, on the pretence of taking her to a party. You said Yes she could go. I took her to an empty house in Westchester I had already picked out. When we got there, I told her to remain outside. She picked wild flowers. I went upstairs and stripped all my clothes off. I knew if I did not I would get her blood on them. When all was ready I went to the window and called her. Then I hid in a closet until she was in the room. When she saw me all naked she began to cry and tried to run down stairs. I grabbed her and she said she would tell her mama. First I stripped her naked. How she did kick – bite and scratch. I choked her to death then cut her in small pieces so I could take my meat to my rooms, cook and eat it. How sweet and tender her little ass was roasted in the oven. It took me 9 days to eat her entire body. I did not **** her, though, I could of [sic] had I wished. She died a virgin.'

(145) Ed Gein was found to have cut off the lips of a dead woman and pinned them on his kitchen blinds.

(146) After he escaped from prison and made his way to

Florida, the authorities didn't have the faintest idea where Ted Bundy was. He could have remained undetected for years if his compulsive urge to kill hadn't got the better of him. Bundy survived by stealing credit cards.

(147) When he was arrested, Dennis Nilsen had a skull wrapped in a plastic bag inside his tea chest.

(149) Richard Ramirez was a big fan of the Marvel comics character Iron Man. He used to do a lot of Iron Man sketches in prison.

(150) Richard Chase used to balance an orange on his head in the mistaken belief that this was a good way to absorb Vitamin C.

(151) Dennis Nilsen and Jeffrey Dahmer both had the same favourite tipple. They were both partial to rum & coke.

(152) Ed Kemper turned himself in shortly after murdering his mother. When he killed he always imagined he was really killing her. Now that his mother was dead this fantasy no longer had any currency.

(153) In 2009 a serial killer named The Phantom of Heilbronn was linked to several murders and many crimes. However, it turned out contaminated DNA swabs had been confused and that in reality there was no Phantom of Heilbronn serial killer at all.

(154) After his arrest, Dennis Nilsen resigned from his position as a civil servant to save the department of employment from any embarrassment while he was awaiting his trial. To be honest, it's not as if he was likely to go back to work anyway. He had already confessed to several murders!

(155) In 1987, the serial killer Randall Woodfield filed a $12 million libel suit against author Ann Rule, the author who wrote a book about him called The I-5 Killer. Woodfield was

angry that the book suggested he'd had herpes and wasn't very intelligent. The Federal Court in Oregon dismissed the lawsuit in January 1988.

(156) The two places in the United States with the least amount of serial killer activity and serial killer murders are Hawaii and South Dakota.

(157) When the police searched Dennis Nilsen's flat after his arrest they found a number of music cassette tapes. Nilsen was fond of The Stranglers - which was bleakly ironic to say the least.

(158) Joel Rifkin was once sent to the solitary wing in prison for getting into an argument with another inmate over who had killed the most people.

(159) When he was released from the Atascadero State Hospital at the age of 21, Edward Kemper was involved in an accident when his motorcycle was struck. He ended up with $15,000 in compensation. In hindsight, this was a dark twist of fate because now he could finally purchase a car - which gave him the ability to pick up hitchhikers.

(160) Killers who were born under a full moon include Edward Kemper, Peter Sutcliffe, and Colin Ireland.

(161) The electric chair was first used in 1890. When one is in the electric chair a surge of 2,000 volts stops the heart and makes you pass out.

(162) Dennis Nilsen liked to put makeup on his victims to hide the post-mortem discolouration.

(163) Randall Woodfield once shot a cleaner named Lisa Garcia at an office building in Oregon. Miraculously, despite being shot in the head, she survived. Garcia was able to testify against Woodfield at his trial.

(164) When he was a suspect in the Green River Murders in the early 1980s, Gary Ridgeway passed a lie detector test so the police wrongly assumed he was innocent.

(165) Kathy Kleiner, who survived Ted Bundy's attack on the Florida University Chi Omega sorority house, never went back to the college to finish her studies. When she picked up her belongings from the dorm a week later she noticed there was still blood on the wall.

(166) According to a study, only 1.5% of serial killer victims were axed to death.

(167) Angelo Buono Jr knew a number of police officers. He would chat to them sometimes during the Hillside Stranglers case.

(168) An FBI agent named Patty Rust had to spend days in David Parker Ray's motor home to catalogue his crimes as The Toy-Box Killer. She was so distressed by the experience she shot herself.

(169) In 1969, Peter Sutcliffe was spoken to by the police after he hit a prostitute over the head with a stone. Sutcliffe was fortunate because the woman did not want to take the matter any further or press charges.

(170) After he killed his victims, Anthony Hardy would dress them in a Demon mask and Mr Men child's socks and take photographs.

(171) Ed Gein was found to have some human skulls on the posters of his bed.

(172) When the police arrested Albert Fish, medical x-rays showed that he had stuck dozens of needles into his genitals.

(173) The address of John Wayne Gacy was 8213 W. Summerdale Ave. A new house was built on the site after the

old one was demolished. You can buy the house that stands there now for about $459,000.

(174) In order to abuct women from parks, Ted Bundy would wear tennis clothes as if he had just stepped off the court. He would also pretend that he had a sailing boat. The police said that Bundy even put on a fake 'British' accent to make himself sound polite and urbane to victims.

(175) The police who had to dig up the garden where Dennis Nilsen lived at Melrose Avenue found a decomposing foot still in a sock in one spot.

(176) Ted Bundy asked for his ashes to be scattered in the same forest where he disposed of many of his victims. His request was actually granted.

(177) China is alleged to have so-called mobile 'execution vans' to save the expense of transporting condemned prisoners.

(178) Leonarda Cianciulli said that she gave away the bars of soap she turned her last victim into as gifts and they proved very popular.

(179) Unbelievably, when Graham Young got a job in a laboratory after his release from a criminal institution the authorities never bothered to tell the lab that Young was a convicted poisoner!

(180) When she decided to become a 'Baby Farmer', Amelia Dyer wrote the following advert offering her services - 'I should be glad to have a dear little baby girl, one I could bring up and call my own. First I must tell you we are plain, homely people, in fairly good circumstances. We live in our own house. I have a good and comfortable home. We are out in the country and sometimes I am alone a good deal. I do not want a child for money's sake but for company and home comfort. Myself and my husband are dearly fond of children. I have no child of my own. A child with me will have a good home and a

mother's love and care. We belong to the Church of England. Although I want to bring the child up as my own, I should not mind the mother or any other person coming to see the child at any time. It would be a satisfaction to see and know the child was getting on all right. I only hope we can come to terms.'

(181) One of the victims of Fred West was the cousin of the novelist Martin Amis.

(182) Amelia Dyer is sometimes suggested as someone who could have been Jack the Ripper but this seems unlikely.

(183) The singer Debbie Harry claimed that she once narrowly escaped getting picked up by Ted Bundy. Her story is not regarded to be credible though as Bundy was in a different area of the country at the time and her description of his car was wrong.

(184) Dennis Nilsen was an excellent chef from his time in the Army Catering Corps but those that knew him said he never used his oven and subsisted on takeaways.

(185) The FBI use Richard Chase as a case study when they teach rookie agents about 'disorganised' serial killers.

(186) Albert Fish once cut off the genitals of a teenager named Thomas Keddon and left him bleeding and tied up in a farmhouse.

(187) Macabre memento hunters chipped pieces of Ed Gein's gravestone off to take away and keep.

(188) When he acted as his own lawyer in court, Ted Bundy tried to file a motion to have the court lunch menu expanded.

(189) In 1972, Caroline Owens was hired as a babysitter by Fred and Rose West. She said she blacked out and woke up to find Fred West binding her with tape. She escaped and went to

the police but they didn't seem to believe her story. Fred West escaped a harsh sentence because Owens was so scared of him she refused to take the Wests to court.

(190) Dennis Nilsen used to put body parts in his garden shed. If anyone mentioned the smell he told them it was compost.

(191) Ted Bundy became a Hindu in prison after his conviction.

(192) A prankster on Twitter once asked Donald Trump to retweet an image of his recently deceased parents. The man said that Donald Trump was a big inspiration to them. The obliging (and vain) Trump retweeted the image - but it was actually of Fred and Rose West! Needless to say, Trump didn't see the funny side and threatened to sue.

(193) People who interviewed Dennis Nilsen or mingled with him in prison say that they never felt uncomfortable in his presence. He never gave off any aura of danger.

(194) Jeffrey Dahmer once drank the spiked drink he had laced for a victim by mistake. He passed out and when he woke up the victim had robbed him and left. Naturally, Dahmer didn't bother to report the crime. The 'thief' had no idea how lucky he had been that Dahmer gave him the wrong drink by mistake.

(195) Carrol Cole actually avoided any charges for murdering his wife. The police assumed she must have got drunk and died of natural causes!

(196) William Suff cooked chilli for fellow workers at office picnics. It is sometimes claimed that he chopped up the body parts of one of his victims and put it in the chilli.

(197) For a few months at the start of 1974, Dennis Nilsen worked in a cafe in Covent Garden.

(198) No one ever found out who Ted Bundy's father was and his mother seemed vague on this question too.

(199) Dennis Radar called his urge to kill 'Factor X'.

(200) One of the strange things about serial killer Donald Henry Gaskins is that he was also a contract killer. You could hire him to kill someone for you.